A JOURNEY INTO THE INVISIBLE

LUCIE LEHOUX

A TRUE STORY

Out of Body Experiences

Other Dimensions, Spiritual Worlds

& Space

A JOURNEY INTO THE INVISIBLE

A Journey into the Invisible

Self-publishing
États-Unis, 2024

ISBN 979-8-9909397-4-5 (paperback)
ISBN 979-8-9909397-5-2 (hardcover)

Original publication in French: July 2024
Une aventure dans l'invisible
© translated by Lucie Lehoux
A Journey into the Invisible: August 2024

© cover designed by Lucie Lehoux (with the help of Discord and Concepts software.)
No other help from artificial intelligence was given to this work.

True story. Certain details in this story, including names, places and dates, have been changed to protect privacy. The content of this story speaks of a possible mental illness, paranormal, supernatural phenomena, spirituality, visions and energies. Be aware that reading may upset you. Therefore, if you are sensitive, surround yourself with people who can help you. If necessary, consult a doctor or other professional services. If expert assistance or counseling is needed, the services of a competent professional should be sought.

The author disclaims any responsibility that this reading may cause.

A parent's consent for the reading of a minor child is recommended.

To my husband, my family, and friends:
THANK YOU for your patience,
your love and support.
I love you very much.

Also, a huge thank you to all those
who helped me in the writing of this book.
I could never have finished it without your help.
Thank you, Edgar, Victor, Shannah and Megan.

Contents

Introduction

Laurie was thirty-five-years-old when, overnight, after opening her chakras and offering a helping hand to the Lord, the confusion between reality and other parallel worlds settled. In her mind, it progressed to such an extent that her loved ones no longer understood her speech and actions, which had become irrational and incomprehensible.

For her, on the contrary, it was quite wonderful and explicable. She had already been initiated briefly into visions, out of body experiences and (on a few occasions) had been in contact with deceased souls. Laurie seemed to be prepared for a more intense travel into the deepest layers of the Universe.

Curious, in search of existential answers, the year 2012 made her travel more than ever into the spiritual world and other dimensions. She did not dwell on whether her supernatural events were the result of mental disorder, or a sudden liberation of her spirit. Laurie allowed herself to be lulled by the wave of the moment.

Preface

Laurie's relatives knew that she didn't like arguments, much less politics, but felt obligated to stay informed on the leaders and their laws. Some knew that she had an interest in spirituality and esotericism. Very few knew about the experiences she had since she was a child with the other world (the world of spirit).

Through her isolated supernatural experiences, Laurie became more and more curious about life and what surrounds the human being in the invisible. Although higher beings such as Mother Mary, archangels, aliens, or visions and past lives seemed taboo subjects to her loved ones, Laurie believed in them. She seemed to be guided to spiritual people working with energies and etheric bodies to assist her journey of learning on these subjects.

From her childhood until her mother's death in the spring of 2008, Laurie had been quietly prepared to open up to these invisible and unknown worlds. She was thirty-one-years-old. Although her mother's death was a sad event, it had been the day she had the opportunity to accompany and see Hetty's soul leave her body and join her deceased parents who were waiting for her in another place.

A week later, on the day of Hetty's burial, alongside the graves of her parents and stillborn little brother, Laurie, her brother Patrick and Hetty's boyfriend had let three doves fly away as a sign of a good start for her. While Hetty's relatives and siblings were also watching the show in the sky, amazingly, four rays of light had appeared from the heavens and positioned themselves at the four corners of the church. This special phenomenon had been considered by all. Some believed that it could be a ray of light for each deceased under the tombstone. For others, it represented a passage for Hetty's soul to go straight to heaven. But no one could have predicted at the time that the number 4 could prophesy that a major event would occur in exactly four years... in the spring of 2012.

For the next year, certain that her mother was still alive in a parallel world, Laurie appreciated her spontaneous visits; Hetty was questioning her about topics that seemed important to her, and Laurie would respond. From these successful contacts, it seemed that Hetty was slowly freeing herself from her ties to the physical world.

On the first anniversary of her death, Laurie had another vision; Hetty was in front of a spiritual master, and she was receiving a kind of diploma. This vision suggested that she was getting permission to travel further into the spirit worlds, and Laurie had believed that she would never see her mother again. Although happy for Hetty, she had cried painfully, as it was difficult for her to tell her loved ones that she was going through a second grieving. A second grief of someone who had already died seemed unrealistic.

Exactly two years had passed since Hetty's passing, and this time Laurie was at the funeral home again for the death of her cousin Steve. She was praying for his soul when, unexpectedly, and in spite of her upright and well-grounded posture, she received a solid invisible thrust in the back that had brought her within a few steps of a gentleman. It was too late to turn back; he'd seen her arrive right next to him. A little embarrassed, unable to find any explanation for what had just happened, Laurie greeted him. Brandon was a friend from work of the deceased. Steve had taught him the functions of delivering newspapers at night. A few days later, Laurie and Brandon had a first date that led them to a romantic relationship. The two had agreed that something weird had happened at the funeral service. Brandon thought it was an invisible push from Steve, Laurie thought it was her mother's, but both were wrong. A year later, they moved in together.

~ 1 ~

She Offered her Help to the Universe

The year 2012 was a time that some people called *the end of the world*, which related to the alignment of the planets, and the end of the Maya calendar. While others would say it will be the year that humanity will have the opportunity to feel and enter into the next dimension.

Uncertain about the future, Laurie was only living in her present moment...

It was the beginning of May 2012. Spring had arrived. Laurie was walking peacefully in her neighborhood before a busy season at work was to begin. She was surprised to see that no one was outside enjoying the beautiful weather. She had taken an energy class a couple weeks ago and she felt inspired. She stopped, looked up at the sky, searched for God's attention and widely opened her chakras. At the first ray shining upon her, she smiled and took a moment to appreciate the great feeling of the sunlight that was already running throughout her entire body. Grateful for His warmth, she was hoping that everyone could feel it, too. It was a pure moment of ecstasy. Searching for justice all her life, she took a solemn position and said silently, *Dear God, Dear Divine, Dear Universe, please, help us, humanity, to reach to another level, where people would be free.* She breathed deeply and added, *to whoever is listening, let me help you. Use me if you need me.*

As she walked back home, feeling lighter than earlier, she noticed there were now a few people outside, finally enjoying their yards. Agreeably surprised of this rapid change in her neighborhood, she wondered if it could be her prayer's answered, but she put that thought quickly behind thinking it was impossible. Instead, she was surprised on the intensity she had put to her prayer mentioning, "use me if you need me."

She was mocking herself when a young man passed by in his white van and distracted her from her thoughts. He stopped and asked, "What are you doing here pretty girl?" She smiled, happy at this attention. It was Brandon, her boyfriend, who was arriving home from a productive meeting with Rosemart, a multinational store that soon will sell his first novel.

***

In the meantime, the number of demonstrations and protestors were increasing in the streets of Montreal. Students, and eventually anybody who felt involved, were also protesting the rise of tuition fees, loan fees and the grant system. Due to thousands of protestors blocking traffic and all of the inconvenience for the businesses in the city, or perhaps to distract the protestors, the Prime Minister and his party had decided to move the meeting with his general council to Aliville.

***

Highly surprised that a major event would occur in her small town, Laurie saw it as a great sign to promote Brandon's novel through this con-gregation. "Babe, we must do something. The release of your book is this weekend, right? These young protesters are a target audience, aren't they? I'm sure many of them would like to read a suspense-horror story. And there will be journalists! And all these people are coming to our little town! And they will gather in the courtyard of Rosemart, exactly the store you signed with to sell your books."

Brandon agreed that this was a great opportunity. And along with two friends, they improvised a stunt.

***

Friday, May 11th, at 3:00 p.m., the temperature felt hot. The courtyard of the store was empty, as the Rosemart store had decided to close before the upcoming event: "The Hight Mass," as one journalist had written.

Laurie and her friend Isabelle were next to the parking lot with a few images of the book cover:

Jesus on a cross facing the Vatican. On the mound behind them, Bran-don and Nicolas quickly installed the big cross and Brandon jumped in to physically reproduce the image of the cover of his book. Somehow, Laurie interpreted Jesus as the peaceful protestors and the Vatican as the government. But once in it, she wondered where she found the courage and the audacity to engage in a publicity stunt like this through such an event.

Dozens of buses began to arrive on Mirabaska Boulevard, and we could see people inside the bus, leaning on the windowsills, pointing and taking pictures and videos of the replica of Jesus on a cross. They were wondering, and Laurie was realizing how this stunt, with a symbol of Christ must have seemed strange for them. She began to experience a rare inner anxiety. She felt that the energy within her immediate vicinity had changed. She felt the people's frustration and animosity related to the confusion of this stunt. Anxious, she was starting to feel physically and morally tired as if she was getting weak. She wasn't sure if she was happy or nervous. She appealed to the Lord and Mary, *Please protect us and put us in Your divine light.*

Many inquisitive minds came to Isabelle and Laurie who were standing next to the parking lot. *Finally,* Laurie thought. They could explain that this scenario was done with the intention of promoting a book from the region. Some showed a little interest, others returned to their group to report the information, others passed rapidly by the girls and went straight up to the mound behind them, as to reach Brandon and Nicolas.

Distressed, Laurie quickly called Nicolas.

"Nicolas! You should get Brandon off the cross. I'm worried. There's a lot of people, and some of them look aggressive!"

"It's fine Laurie! They just want to ask questions. I promise you, if it gets out of hand, I'll get him down."

In the courtyard, there were people putting on their raincoats and getting ready for the march. Some leaders were shouting in a megaphone, either to denounce the increase in tuition fees or to evoke slogans. Laurie was trying to listen, but she was too preoccupied to understand. Isabelle could feel her friend panicking. To help her calm down, she humorously said, "Looks like a photo shoot! It seems they are having a good time taking pictures and videos with Brandon on the cross."

Laurie calmed down some when the organizer had taken control of the megaphone reminding all the people to come to the start line. Many of the people who had spent some time with Brandon and Nicolas were now greeting the girls on their way back to their event. Some were saying this promotion stunt was a good idea, while others seemed to think that it was a waste of time. Exhausted, Laurie just wanted it to be over, but the boys wanted to stay longer. They wanted to continue the show as the potential clientele was gathered at the traffic light further, and soon they would be walking next to them while continuing through the congregation center where the Prime minister meeting was taking place.

Finally, Laurie could breathe. With the splendid sunset she was seeing behind Brandon and the symbol of faith, she was praying that there would be no riots here in her little town. She took a formal position as the protestors walked. When they were out of sight, Isabelle exclaimed as she warmed up herself, "Brandon must be frozen!"

They reached the guys and indeed, Brandon was shivering so much that he had trouble putting on his socks.

When they arrived at home, Laurie instantly fell to her knees. She was exhausted. As the other three were in great shape, they wanted to celebrate and look at videos that may already be shared on social media. Laurie only wanted her bed. But Laurie's rationality will slowly change.

Could it be the stress of the stunt? Or the result of offering the Universe to be used if needed, to help humanity find peace and liberty?

***

At the wee hour, she woke up in a panic. Something was wrong. The moment she gained consciousness, she felt unusually disoriented. She had a strange feeling that her boyfriend, who was lying next to her, was in critical condition and he might be dying. All her focus was on him, and she was waiting for a sign. In the dim light of the early morning, she could see Brandon's body had turned distinctly pale, and a sudden panic grew in her eyes. When she touched and felt how cold his body had become, her consciousness told her to act rapidly. She was already kneeling over him with both her hands in action, rubbing him aggressively in order to bring the

4

circulation back into his body as well as recharge his energy.

With tears in her eyes and while listening to the rhythm of Brandon's erratic breathing, she was rubbing his upper body and praying to the Lord to save his life. Rapidly, she moved her hands to his thighs and continued the rubbing actions, increasing the circulation in his chilled body. Suddenly, a more than welcome calm settled into her. With a renewed feeling of calmness, she suspended her action for a few seconds and wondered if what was happening was real. Nevertheless, because she felt confused, she got up at the foot of the bed and continued massaging his calves and warming his feet—just in case!

Thankfully, Brandon moved his head slowly on his pillow. His breathing changed, and he fortunately seemed to be finally back to normal. *He's saved!* Laurie felt quite proud of herself and the work she had done. It seemed to her she had provided the correct maneuver and saved her boyfriend from dying, but in the next second, she questioned herself again as if he had ever been in danger. Uncertain, she went back to bed thinking she'll ask him later.

~ 2 ~

Brandon Crucified Himself

In the morning, as this good-looking man arrived in the kitchen in great shape, healthy and without any signs of distress, he had no comments about the vigorous massage he received during the night. Laurie was still confused. *Had I hallucinated? Had Brandon really been in danger?*

"Good morning, sweetheart." Laurie said as she was looking for a way to approach the subject. "I made coffee. Would you like some?"

"I'd love some." Brandon answered happily as he reached for a cup.

"Did you notice I gave you a massage last night?"

"Yes, and why did you do that?" he asked with an inquiring look.

"I don't know. I woke up with the feeling that you were getting sick." As usual, unable to hide her thoughts when being ask, she continued, "I saw you turning white, and I just felt I had to rub you to save you from I don't know—maybe from dying."

"Are you serious?" Brandon asked as he seemed doubting.

"Why not?" she said as if she was joking. "Maybe I should congratulate myself for saving your butt! Don't you remember how cold you were last night at the publicity stunt, wearing only a small towel?"

"You're right." Brandon said, approaching closer with a seductive look, ready to kiss her. "Thank you for your rubbing massage. I loved it."

Laurie was pleased but in the back of her head, she was still confused. *Had I hallucinated? If yes, why?* Because Brandon didn't have anything else to add, she chose to put it all behind her and got ready for work.

***

Laurie was working for over fifteen years in an office at the family business that her Aunt Angela and Uncle Peter owned. Alone in the office, between the few calls she received that day, she heard bits of news about last night's demonstration. She also found out another rally continued in the afternoon in front of the Convention Centre. She rarely took days off, but this morning she didn't want to be working. She was restless and had difficulty concentrating. It was sunny outside, and she sincerely wanted to stand for justice and be among the peaceful protestors rather than be holed up in this small dull office. For a change, she wanted to revolt—just a little—and ask for a day off.

After a hard talk, unhappy about having to do her job over his, and especially because the demonstration was involved, Peter finally replied, "Okay, we'll talk on Monday. Are there any special orders that I should know about?"

"No," Laurie said in a haste, "all the orders are taken care of. I'll give you news later."

Happy to have a day off, she quickly left the office, hoping to surprise Brandon at home.

"Hi! I took the day off. Do you want to go to the mobilization?" Visibly surprised to see his girlfriend arriving so early, Brandon accepted as he jumped from the computer chair. But to be sure Laurie knew what to expect, he grabbed the TV controller and put on the news to see what happened last night. It was images of violence; rocks and projectiles such as billiard balls were thrown, grenades of fumes kept exploding, protesters were lying on the ground wounded. Other news channels showed images of politicians inside the Convention Centre looking out the windows at what was happening outside. Some seemed concerned while others seemed to take the situation lightly.

Since the previous evening, Laurie had thought the protest had gone well and that the sign of Faith had brought peace to the meeting. "This is so sad. It's like we are in wartime!" Despite Laurie's disappointment, they got dressed and went to protest the rise in tuition fees.

As they were marching to the meeting point, Laurie had a strange feeling as if she was momentarily detached from her body, as well as an uncanny thought that they were meant to be there together. The main street was closed to motorists that day and the couple was walking in the middle of the road. It was a hot day, the sky was beautiful, and there were only a few clouds. About four black helicopters were flying low over the site.

"I've never seen helicopters getting so close to the ground!" Laurie yelled because of the loud noise of the machines.

"Me neither!" Brandon said quickly, searching for people he may know among the crowd of protestors of all ages, with all kinds of signs of protest about the environment, peace, education, and better public services. This demonstration wasn't exclusively for the students.

Dazzled by the show, Laurie was surprised to feel so open and peaceful. It was as if she was having an out-of-body experience, because in a different way, she could see in people's eyes how much they wanted to be heard, to be free, and to live in a healthy environment. Even if she felt her eyelids were more open than usual, she rationalized this feeling as overexcitement to be off work and that she could enjoy this wonderful day. In this moment, she wasn't worried about this strange change in her. She greeted people and enjoyed the moment.

But suddenly, her state of happiness evaporated as something was starting to annoy her. Strangely, she was feeling discomfort in her body. She started to tremble and circle Brandon. Even though she realized her behavior was odd, she continued. Not wondering what Brandon would think, she was alert to what was going on in the perimeter.

After many circles around Brandon, she stopped and remained frozen. Curious, she looked at buses that arrived further. Police officers had arrived next to the busses and checked the rioter's backpacks as they exited. Once finished, oddly Laurie wasn't feeling the discomfort in her body anymore, as if those emotions belonged to the rioters or the police officers.

Even though she felt better, Laurie asked Brandon if he wanted to leave. He agreed and while leaving the crowd, she asked him if he saw the group of people that got off the bus. Brandon had seen it, so Laurie added, "Looks like they've played paintball... Have you seen the color marks on the clothes?" He didn't notice.

Later, on the radio, it had been said that when the protesters had left the city of Aliville, the squads had stopped the buses and asked to see everyone's legs. In fact, during the two demonstrations, snipers had discerned the vandalizers from the protesters, and they marked them by shooting them with paintballs. The impact of the balls had left bruises on them. Therefore, those with trademarks became easily identifiable and would be charged and arrested for vandalism. Laurie found this idea to be genius even if some rioters thought it was abuse.

Back at home, later in the afternoon, Laurie had an inexplicable sensation of being light, powerful and deeply in love. Her new feelings were extraordinarily well-defined. She felt like Brandon and her understood each other like never before. When they made love she realized she had a more developed sense of touch than usual. She had the impression they were in another dimension, but never wondered about her condition; it was simply right and natural.

Her feeling of deepness faded away as she heard her cell phone ring. She wiped away her happy tears and answered joyfully to Peter. In an angry tone (a tone she had not often heard coming from him) he asked her if she took care of all the orders she received in the morning before she left for the peaceful protest. Laurie snapped back even more to reality when she remembered one, she hadn't. It was her first oversight of this kind.

Laurie apologized, "No. I completely forgot about one. I'm sorry. Did I tell you that I was having a hard time concentrating this morning? I know that's not an excuse, but please excuse me."

"We will talk on Monday," Peter quickly replied. He softened his tone when he added that mistakes happen.

Laurie told Brandon about the incident with Peter. He suggested watching a TV show so she could forget about it. Finally calm and with her head resting on the back of the couch, Laurie listened, more or less, to what was happening on the TV. She was slightly intrigued by the images which were sometimes blurry and sometimes in 3D. It was as if the actors were right there in the living room. She wasn't concerned about what she was seeing being illogical or irrational. In fact, when her eyes finally focused on the images and her gullible mind accepted what originally appeared fantastical, she was wondering why the show was so successful despite such a self-centered main character.

As a result of this question and the strange images before her, her mind retreated elsewhere. As the couple went to bed, her mind was still elsewhere.

It was the middle of the night, and Laurie hadn't fallen asleep since she laid down beside her boyfriend, which was only a few hours ago. She assumed it was due to insomnia. After one of those brief moments of drowsiness, an incredible and unthinkable idea became clear to her. Recalling everything that had happened since Friday night—Brandon's standing on a cross in front of a crowd, then last night Brandon dying next to her, and now, the weird feeling she sensed in the room that Brandon was somehow between two worlds—made her believe that something great was happening. Her gullible mind didn't question any irrationality. With those recollections, she believed that Brandon, like Jesus did according to the Bible, had been crucified, had died and was now in the process of a resurrection.

Laurie's body reacted with a sudden jolt. Lying on her back, her body was stiff as a statue. She was holding her breath, and her eyes were open more than needed due to the darkness of the room. She was surprised and happy at the same time. A smile grew on her face. She felt pampered and proud of being his girlfriend. She was seeing the images scrolling instantly and strongly. Thus, she believed her sweetheart had done this amazing sacrifice for the good of everyone involved with the protest. *He had crucified himself for all of humankind.*

Because she accepted and integrated this new reasoning into her consciousness, images of gods and goddesses comfortably lying on clouds, watching the human species were shown to her. Somehow, she understood that there was other Beings, living in another world parallel to hers, separated by a simple invisible veil. She imagined that this impressive feat of Brandon's resurrection had a true purpose for them—as if there had been a link created between the physical world and the spiritual world. *Who can tell?*

With a satisfied smile, she cherished the thought and tried to fall asleep, but it was in vain. Her mind was so busy floating around with blurry ideas that she wasn't worried about her unusual lack of concentration during the day, or her few out-of-body experiences. In fact, she was trying to remember what she knew about Jesus's crucifixion, His story, the Bible, Catholicism.

As far as she could remember that night, she was about 4-years-old when she learned about the existence of Jesus. It was December the 24th. Her dad's extended family were gathering at her uncle's house. She was playing with her cousins and suddenly they had to stop and put on their winter coats to go to church, for the midnight mass, and celebrate Jesus' birthday as she was told. By the time they arrived, she was sleeping, and her dad took her in his arms. Inside the building she felt so good. She felt at peace. She loved the serenity of the place and hearing the adults telling each other their best wishes. She saw the excitement in her older cousins' eyes because soon after they would open their Christmas gifts. She loved the stained glass on the windows, and the statue of Mary with her arms opened. Laurie also sent her best wishes to baby Jesus, the One they were celebrating.

When she was about six-years-old, her grandfather (on her father's side) had passed away, and her mom asked her and her brother to say a prayer for their grandfather's soul. She had lost her own dad a few years prior and she believed his soul was still alive, somewhere in the sky. When Laurie showed her a picture of Jesus that she had somewhere among her old drawings, she asked her mother if she should send her prayer to Him, Hetty said, "Either to him or to God, as long as you feel good with who you pray at." Laurie's mother didn't want to talk about Catholicism since she didn't want to interfere with her husband's belief. Stephane used to believe in the Catholic Church, but when he had learned about the atrocity of pedophilia that some priests had done to some children, he avoided going to church. So, despite her own belief, Hetty rarely asked her children to pray.

A little later, Laurie had been introduced to Catholicism. She was sev-en-years-old, during her second grade, and while in the schoolyard, Laurie felt attracted by a girl of her age who was sitting on a tree trunk waiting for the bus. Laurie had approached Arianne who instantly became her best friend. Arianne's parents were catholic and Laurie had prayed with them a few times. There were times that Laurie had slept over and on Sundays, she had the choice to go to Church with her family, or be brought back home. Wanting to spend more time with her friend, even if her parents didn't totally believe in the Catholic Church, they accepted their daughter would attend Church with Arianne and her family. Every time, she felt in-credibly good and feverish in that holy place. However, as the two friends got older, they were allowed to sit on the last bench alone, away from the family, and they wouldn't pay too much attention to the Sunday sermons. Eventually, they simply didn't have to attend church anymore.

In fact, Laurie had not learned much about the Bible or all the teach-ings. She had been baptized and confirmed, but instead of receiving a religious education, she found her own spiritual beliefs in God, Jesus, Mother Mary, and the deceased. Like her mom, she believed her grandpar-ents were somewhere in the sky.

~ 3 ~

A Dimension Where Time Doesn't Exist

Sunday morning, May 13, 2012

The sun finally rose. Laurie felt weak; she was hardly able to clean herself up; she barely had breakfast; she felt drained from all those thoughts and those sleepless nights.

The phone rang and she answered with difficulty. It was Arianne, her best friend, who wanted to know what had happened on Friday. "I saw videos of Brandon on the cross during the demonstration. I didn't think you would do that kind of presentation!" Arianne had been surprised because she knew her friend was typically a shy person.

Laurie was having trouble concentrating, but explained, "It went so fast! We had the idea of putting a cross like Brandon's book cover, but at the last-minute, Brandon was on it!" Arianne detected a little exasperation in her friend's tone of voice and generously offered to do something to help. Laurie responded in a warm and appreciative tone that she would call her later. As soon as they said goodbye, Laurie felt a need to physically move. Her body was not feeling well. Did she need to throw up? Not sure. Did she need to sleep? Probably. She felt her entire body was filled with anxiety. She immediately went to her bedroom and walked in circles while practicing concentrated breathing in order to calm down.

Brandon was in the kitchen doing the dishes while Laurie was in the room standing in front of the patio door. She was crying and asked silently for help: *Lord, please help me!*

Remarkably, a few seconds later, Laurie felt that her deceased mother was there to calm her down. Using her energy, Hetty touched her dear daughter in a marvelous way from the back of her head to the back of her ankles while encouraging her to breathe. She also whispered in her ear—or more directly into her thoughts—"Call Tim!"

Laurie didn't realize it had been three years since her mom's last special visit. She simply thought: *Yes, he will know what to do to help me!*

Tim was a psychic that Laurie had met about five months prior. It was during a consultation with a dozen close friends of her dead cousin Steve, who had passed about nineteen months prior to that time. Brandon and Judy, the widow of Steve, had invited this psychic who was well known for his clairvoyant gift. Apparently, through the soul of Steve, Tim could answer each one's secret questions. Mostly by curiosity, Laurie had agreed to participate in this meeting. When it was Laurie's turn to meet privately with Tim, she sat in front of him, smiled and waited for his lead. He smiled timidly and asked what she wanted to know. Deep inside, Laurie wanted to know if the few interactions with her mom since her death had been real, but instead she secretly asked, "How is my cousin Steve doing?" After a moment, Tim smiled and said nothing. He was looking intensely at Laurie like he wanted her to feel what was happening in the room. Laurie became fascinated with what seemed to be a thin substance moving on her right side at the ceiling height. As she was attentive to it, she felt a strong sensation as if an invisible being was asking her if she was ready. *Yes,* she said silently. Then, that thin substance vanished, and astonishingly, Laurie was seeing her cousin's etheric body.

Steve was clearly expressing happiness through his beautiful smile and his piercing blue eyes that were looking directly at her. In this extraordinary different, visible energy, like a sixth sense, Laurie sensed he was disappointed thinking he had died too soon, but he was working on accepting it. He knew about all the prayers she asked for him and he was grateful for it. She felt that he was proud of his little cousin for being able to see him, and then she sensed he hugged her tenderly before that special moment came to an end. Laurie swept her tears as she asked Tim, "Did you see him, too?" Before answering, Tim gave her a moment to completely return from her emotions and said that he was not allowed to see, but he felt a positive connection between her and another presence. Excited, Laurie told him it was her cousin Steve and continued, "To be honest, I wanted to know if all those interactions I had experienced with another world were real. And the contact with my cousin's soul today was exactly what I needed as an answer."

Tim encouraged her to believe in her gut, saying she was probably an empath. Laurie smiled, having no idea what he was talking about at that time. Later, when they all sat around the table and shared each other's experiences, Uncle Peter, apparently happily surprised by his own experience, asked Tim how he was doing what he was doing. Tim laughed, seemingly pleased for this day, and replied with self-confidence, "You are all capable of doing it, too, if you wish to." He added that he was going to give courses on energy here in Aliville in the coming weeks. Uncle Peter and Laurie were the only ones in that group who went to the first meeting. Then Laurie was the only one who continued the few courses that Tim provided to a small group. Throughout those classes, she learned about energy transfer and chakras. Between that moment and the student protests, Laurie had practiced those techniques a few times alone.

Following her mom's advice, Laurie went to her drawer to find Tim's phone number. She called her previous energy teacher, and as the phone rang she hoped that he would answer, that he would remember her, and above all, that he could help her.

"Hi Tim. It's Laurie from Aliville!" She said while looking at her forced smile in the mirror.

Tim responded immediately with a warm tone and asked how she was doing.

She felt a bit relieved, and curiously felt like he anticipated her call. "Actually, not very well. I'm having trouble breathing. I feel dizzy."

Tim was waiting at the other end of the line, waiting for more information. Laurie was trying to find the right words.

"Where can I go to GET GROUNDED? I need to BE CONNECTED TO THE EARTH!"

There was a moment of silence. Tears were welling in her eyes and she had a lump in her throat that made it difficult to speak. But also, she needed more time before continuing because she was so confused as to why the words "get grounded" and "connect to the earth" came out of her mouth faster than her thoughts. Moments before she dialed his number, she thought that he would more than likely tell her to breathe into a paper bag to calm her anxiety. But now, it was making more sense. She needed to be reconnected to the earth.

"I feel myself disconnecting from the boundaries of earth. I'm not feeling well."

After a short while, when Tim could understand her needs, he replied, "Normally, a good way to recharge is to go near a water pond. Is that possible for you?"

As the word "pond" resonated into her ear, Laurie already had thought of two options. She could already see herself at the lake near Arianne's parents' home, and the next second, next to the pond on Uncle Peter and Aunt Angela's estate. She had never experienced anything like that before and didn't realize it was special.

Focused, she questioned, "Do I have to get into the water?"

Tim seemed amused, and replied, "No, you just need to be close to it."

At this confirmation, she felt thankful because the water was still cold in the beginning of May.

Satisfied, standing in front of the mirror, she checked her appearance and said, "Thanks, Tim. I found the perfect place to go to."

"It was my pleasure," Tim said before ending the call.

Laurie was looking at her reflection when, in an unexpected way, her soul flew over her uncle's land. Her soul was no longer in her room—she was standing in front of the water pond, but there were no buildings or roads around. The ground was dry, the dirt was kind of red, and Laurie was having difficulty breathing. She shook her head and frowned in disbelief. *What is happening to me? Where am I?* Then just like that, she was standing in front of an empty lake. It seemed as if someone had waited until Laurie was ready to venerate and delight in what was to follow...

The earth began to move and transformed as if it was the beginning of creation. In front of her, this landscape was changing at the speed of light, going from a dry area to a flooded area. Water began to flow. In the blink of an eye, the vegetation was growing. Laurie was quite dazzled to see small, green plant shoots and trees growing and flourishing freely, allowing themselves to be lulled by the wind. In this newly formed lake, marine life was created; the colors of each species were beautiful, pure and vivid. Then, very quickly, sea creatures started crawling out of the water. Some became lizards, others into mammals, until some morphed into the human species.

At one point, while she was witnessing the evolution of mankind, an apparition of Jesus's etheric body appeared and stood beside the pond. This was a strange event as He never moved while everything else was changing and evolving. This great vision and the feeling that she had deep inside made her believe that even before the human species evolved in throughout time, He was there blessing the land and all that was created.

The phenomena ended and she was back in her present time. Her soul was back in her body, in her bedroom, looking at herself in the mirror of her dresser. Even though she supposed it was unrealistic, she was amazed: *Wow! I'm really lucky to have had... this moment?... Vision?... Message?*

Barely intrigued, Laurie didn't question why and how this phenomenon came to be. She was just grateful to have lived this moment; to have seen in a marvelous way these wonderful ancient images of how life had been created on earth. She reserved a special chamber in her mind to remember it all: what she saw, what she felt, and what she believed it was.

Still looking at her reflection, in a rather gallant way, she embraced her sincere smile, put her right leg behind her left, bowed a little forward, lowering her eyes towards the ground, took a deep breath to appreciate this moment of pure silliness and then exclaimed, "Thank you, Lord, for this special moment!"

As she rose up from her bow, she felt an invisible thrust in her chest that caused her to step back. It was strong enough to make her realize that something had pushed her, but not strong enough to hurt or frighten her. Laurie paused a moment to listen, to understand what had just happened.

After five seconds had passed, she smiled again. She understood the theory of time traveling! She had traveled into time. *Time is relative!* Albert Einstein and others before her had explained this remarkable phenomenon, and she advantageously experienced a brief overview.

"I did it!" she exclaimed, not wondering why it happened to her.

Recovering from her emotion, Laurie called Uncle Peter and asked if she could stop by. She confessed that she wanted to get some fresh air and go near the pond. Without any hesitation, Uncle Peter told her she was always welcome. She informed Brandon where she was going, and surprisingly, he wanted to join her.

~ 4 ~

Laurie's Experiences Before 2012

When Laurie was seventeen-years-old, she encountered her first supernatural experience. She was a teenager, and everything seemed to be perfect in her life. She had good health, a family who loved her, she was surrounded by good friends, everything went well at school. But she often felt anxious, and she wondered why.

One day, exhausted by this annoying feeling, Laurie turned for the first time to the Universe and asked for answers. Due to her request, overnight, mysterious phenomenon began happening to her. She felt invaded by black spots surrounding her. Surprised, she wondered, *What is that?* Each time they reappeared, Laurie tried to ignore them, but more scary black spots were around her. Her anxiety grew as she perceived those black spots to be evil souls. Their presence had made her feel weak, sad, and frightened. She had prayed, and the thought of calling a man she knew entered her mind. A man that was working with energy. Gratefully, she had been guided toward this shaman who practiced energy healing and energy balancing on her.

At that time, weirdly and unlike most of her friends, Laurie believed in this kind of healing. During her treatment, she was lying on her back, on a massage table, in the middle of a room that served as an office. Hundreds of books and several documents were evident in the room. The healer played relaxing music, and the air was filled with the smell of incense. Several candles lit up the room as Mr. Normand stood to her right, seeming to be in a trance. Laurie's eyes were partially open for a few moments while he demonstrated Indian ritual-like movements with his hands. He whispered words Laurie could barely hear. This was her first visit and she felt as if he was practicing an invocation on her. Tears had started to flow. She was seeing them again—images of evil souls flying around her, trying to frighten her with their intimidating faces and their demonic laughter. Lau-

21

rie had prayed to repel them, to make them disappear.

Amazingly, on the other side of Mr. Normand, she saw an energy that resembled a spiritual guide. She paid attention and thought it could be a guardian angel. *Are you my guardian angel?* Still in a trance, Mr. Normand didn't seem to see the energy. To validate, inwardly, Laurie had asked him his name– "Raphael" immediately came to her mind. Thinking it was his guardian angel, she felt a bit calmer, as those dreadful energies were still floating around in large numbers. Laurie had continued to pray, like Carmen, her best friend's mother had taught her. "I greet you Mary, full of grace..." Then, miraculously, without ever being able to imagine such an apparition, Mother Mary appeared instantly. She was graciously standing up at the tip of Laurie's head who was lying down on the table. In a gentle but powerful gesture, Mother Mary had opened her arms horizontally and swept the evil souls out of Laurie's etheric space. She saw herself surrounded by a pure white light. Laurie was witnessing the remaining evil souls that were now disappearing like magic.

Even though everything was real, for a moment, Laurie had wondered about this possibility. *Is it possible Mother Mary is here with me?* The feminine energy who was still behind Laurie's head, had kept her arms open and was offering her protection through light. She had the same delicate veil and expressed the same grace as the images of the Mother Mary's statue she had seen a few times in church. Laurie had convinced herself, *who else could it be? Who else has the power and grace to do that?* Mother Mary was there to protect her when she needed her help so badly. She had come into darkness to free her from these demonic spirits and pushed away those evil souls from Laurie's etheric body. Laurie thanked her with all her heart for her presence, her protection, and her light. Even though she felt more secure, she asked Mary to stay a while longer. Laurie was afraid her protector would leave too soon, and the evil spirits would appear again.

Fortunately, Mother Mary had stayed. Laurie closed her eyes, felt herself surrounded by pure light, and quietly these entities departed. It was as if Mother Mary had forbidden them to re-enter into Laurie's energy space again. She had protected Laurie, freed her, and wrapped her in her loving arms. As Laurie felt Mother Mary's energy depart, her fear had dissipated as well.

When the treatment with Mr. Normand had ended, Laurie felt incredibly relieved, and on his part, Mr. Normand seemed satisfied with his own revelation. She told him about her vision of the guardian angels. He told her that he had felt several presences, but nothing more. He changed the subject to one that bothered him a lot lately.

A meteorite heading straight to our planet. He had explained to Laurie that people like him, with their energy, were trying to deflect the meteorite. Although Laurie had listened attentively, it was only two days later that she believed in his story and in the strength of energy forces. It had been discreetly announced on the radio that we had just avoided a meteorite which could have destroyed planet earth.

After experiencing this amazing event, Laurie shared her experience with Arianne, but at this time, both friends had different opinions as to what could have been the reason of this phenomenon; the idea of Catholicism and other ways of healing. Arianne had been educated in goodness and received religious teachings. Because her mother Carmen was working as a nurse in a hospital, they both believed more in science than the effect of energy that surrounds us, and the healing of medication instead of energy treatment. To avoid probable unwanted criticism from her other friends, Laurie had kept this secret with Mother Mary well buried in her heart. At that age, with the many friends she had, sharing this kind of phenomenon would probably have done her more harm than good. At peace with herself, Laurie acknowledged that obscure entities cannot survive in the divine light, so, in her relationship with others, she looked for light over obscurity.

***

Laurie was a young adult when her maternal grandmother passed away. Standing next to her mom, as they both looked at her in the coffin, Laurie had a strange feeling that her grandmother was still alive despite her inanimate body. She felt the deceased playful like she was hiding and could talk to her at any time. Laurie shared her thoughts with her mother, and Hetty was thinking the same.

A few times throughout the following months, while walking alone outside, for no particular reason, Laurie had an apparition of her grandmother. Marie-Ange had appeared in the sky above. Laurie was drawn to the image, and saw her short, semi-curly, white hair which perfectly framed her affectionate blue eyes and her warm smile. Laurie was seeing her grandmother's upper etheric body and her shoulders bouncing up and down because she was still laughing wholeheartedly like she used to. After this first vision, Laurie had doubted a phenomenon like this could be real. On the second similar vision, Marie-Ange was laughing wholeheartedly because of the look on her granddaughter's face, wondering if what she was seeing was real. Then, on the third apparition, an inexplicable contact had been created between the two of them. Following that experience, each time Laurie had a thought about her grandmother, Marie-Ange would appear spontaneously, smiling and bigger-than-life in the sky.

***

When Laurie was about twenty-one-years-old, she was still surrounded by good friends, had a good job and she was a new homeowner with her dear boyfriend Philippe. One afternoon, for no explicable reason, she perceived visions that left her frightened. Whether her eyes were open or closed, the lights on or off, her head under the comforter or not, and whether she wanted to or not, she was seeing images of carnage/barbary; it was men from another epoque with armors, killing each other with axes and swords. Laurie was so anxious that Philippe thought Laurie was perhaps possessed, or she was somehow suddenly exhibiting the behavior of a clairvoyant. In order to help her, he went downstairs and returned with the crucifix wall cross.

The more she wanted to avoid or deny those images, the more the visions became violent and bloody. Laurie was afraid, *But why do I see these images?* She prayed and Lisa came to her mind. Lisa was her good friend, older but spiritual, and she liked to talk freely about energy healing. The next day Laurie went her, and as wise advice, Lisa had told her to look at the scary visions without judgement, allow them to be, let them pass through the body and give herself permission to freely feel all emotions that may arise within her, and then let them go. Coincidently or not, that night Laurie saw on TV images of barbary-like visions that she had over the last 24 hours. She became interested in the movie based on a legend of seven knights on their horses fighting against an army of Saxons who were invading Rome, which occurred during the 7th century. Arthur and his knights went to war because they had been manipulated by a bishop with bad intentions. In a remote village, another man with high authority was bringing hunger and punishment to the people just to show them he was superior. He wrongly preached in the name of God.

Seeing those scenes, Laurie felt deeply for Arthur as he fought for justice and freedom; strongly putting down the tyrant man. He pushed the tyrant out of his way, freed the prisoner, and spoke up confidently, "With my God, every man here was born free." After watching that movie, Laurie's own visions of barbary were still appearing. She followed her friend's advice and paid attention to the images without judging. From this exercise, she sadly understood those visions might be her own memories of a past life. *Could I have been involved in a war? Could I have lived a past life?* It was almost impossible. Nevertheless, as she allowed the visions to pass through her, without judgment as Lisa advised, she then felt as if they were her own memories. She felt that she had been physically involved in a war among plenty of other souls, hundreds of years ago.

Incredibly, at that moment, Laurie felt the collective sadness and pain of every warrior. She burst into tears as she allowed the emotion to live one last time, realizing that those memories wanted to be freed and forgiven. Seeing herself committing those violent acts, Laurie cried and yelled for hours; trying to accept and absolve herself from any such bloodshed and killings she had committed in a previous life.

The next day of this revelation, exhausted but at peace, the disturbing visions had faded away. From this experience, those visions never returned. Laurie was convinced she had lived a past life, and by accepting and forgiving herself she had been healed.

When Laurie thanked her friend Lisa for her great advice, strangely Lisa couldn't remember saying that, but recognized it to be the best way to release memories of a past life. Even though Philippe and Laurie had kept that incident quite secret from friends and family, a few times Laurie had tried to talk about past life, reincarnation and mental problems related to those topics. But most of her close friends didn't believe or didn't want to talk about those taboo subjects.

***

About one year later, Philippe and Laurie had decided to break up and to sell the house. While she was resting on the bed in the guest room, sad but looking to find peace within her, Laurie had a special experience; spontaneously, her mind left her body and stunningly, her mind was floating in the air. Mechanically she looked down. She saw many people standing up, all in line, individually separated by four high and narrow walls. The walls were so high that it seemed to be the reason why the men were unable to communicate with each other. Floating above, higher up, Laurie quickly saw her best friend Arianne and shouted, "Look Ari, I'm here, in the air! Look up Ari!" But Arianne didn't hear her and instantly, Laurie returned to her body. Surprised by this phenomenon, Laurie understood the images of the four walls to be a representation of the brain, and inexplicably, she had been able to free herself from it for a moment.

She told her mom about that phenomenon. Because Hetty had experienced something similar, she understood someone could somehow have an out of body experience. And yet she had seriously warned her daughter not to force the events because it could be dangerous for her. From this advice, Laurie rarely forced manifestation, but was more and more curious about those phenomena she experienced.

***

26

In 2007 Laurie had a new boyfriend, Miguel. After a few months, Miguel had difficulty breathing, and he had asked Laurie to go with him for holistic healing. Laurie was surprised to know that his family had indigenous roots and they often turned to holistic treatment for physical pain.

Sitting next to her boyfriend, Laurie had met Mrs. Hélène for the first time. The lady was in her forties and had left the hospital environment because she preferred practicing non-conventional medicine. Mrs. Hélène was more about healing people with herbs, or by cleaning their etheric body. And when it was appropriate, she preferred healing from the source.

She had said to her client, "There is someone, an entity around you who wants to help you, but he is holding you too tight, and that's the reason you can't breathe freely. Do you know who it could be? I will ask him to leave you now." A few hours later, like magic, Miguel was breathing much better.

Several weeks later, Laurie had met Mrs. Hélène, hoping to learn more about existential questions, about life, and what is around us. Mrs. Hélène was generous, especially when she shared her knowledge about the difference between the physical body and etheric body. In that moment, Laurie felt a strange energy behind her back. She looked at it and amazingly, she saw the head of a dragon. Despite her surprise, she took the time to look carefully at it; the beast was calm and seemed to be listening to Mrs. Hélène's explanations. Laurie continued to listen to the lady while admiring, incomprehensively without fear, the vision of a dragon who seemed to be living in light years but was in Laurie's etheric body as Mrs. Hélène explained. Fascinated, Laurie watched each of the creature's movements; when he was blinking his eyes or when he was moving and searching for a better position.

When Mrs. Hélène was done with her long explanation, she asked Laurie if she had other questions. Laurie had asked her if it was possible that a dragon was behind her back, in her etheric body. Spontaneously, the lady had laughed and told Laurie she didn't know if it was a dragon, but she had confirmed she had felt a presence and asked it to leave Laurie's etheric body. Mrs. Hélène finished the appointment by concluding that what happens in the etheric body belongs to another dimension, often unseen by the human eye.

After this experience, Laurie had a new conviction; that dragons truly existed, but she wondered if they were still alive in another dimension or if her vision was from the memory of a past life. At this moment it time, thinking she will never find out the truth, Laurie simply read on Chinese horoscope and when it was appropriate, she liked to admit she had been born under the dragon sign.

At another session, Mrs. Hélène had suggested to Laurie to read the book *Jonathan Livingston Seagull* by the author Richard Back. The story recounts the evolution of Jonathan, a seagull who was passionate about flying higher and faster to be free. He believed that there was much more to do than just use his wings to fly close to shore and catch fish for food. Throughout her reading, Laurie understood a little bit more about the difference between the physical world and the spiritual world.

There was a passage that told the story of Jonathan. One day, he had met with a spiritual guide who had told him, "Your soul allows you to see what you're able to see." That quote comforted her as to the reason why she was seeing what she was seeing. This reading helped her to believe more in the possibility of a parallel world separated by a simple small veil.

***

In the spring of 2008, Laurie's mother passed away. Of course, it was a sad day, but throughout this event, Hetty had given her daughter the wonderful gift of not being afraid of death; there was an afterlife. Beyond belief, Laurie saw her mother's soul leaving her body and passing from this life to another place where her dead grandparents were waiting for her. Marie-Ange and William were waiting patiently in a place that seemed to be parallel to our world, but simply hidden behind a veil. Since that phenomenon, Laurie wasn't afraid of death, or the unknown. In order to preserve this magical moment, Laurie had chosen carefully the people that she could talk with about her visions and her phenomena.

Then, exactly two years to the date, in the spring of 2010, Laurie met

Brandon, her boyfriend. It was at her cousin Steve's funeral service and Laurie had received a firm invisible thrust that drove her within two steps of Brandon. Many months later, Brandon was the one who had presented Laurie to Tim, the psychic. On that same day Laurie had a special interaction with her dead cousin Steve. Following that event, Laurie had taken a few classes with Tim on energy and chakras.

~ 5 ~
Craziness or an Opening of the 3rd Eye?

Laurie was silent in the car with Brandon while on their way to Uncle Peter's property. She was thinking about the previous phenomenon she just experienced in her bedroom: the vision on the evolution of Earth, the vision about Jesus and the understanding of space-time.

Once they arrived, Laurie and Brandon showed Aunt Angela and Uncle Peter videos and pictures of their stunt during the manifestation on Friday evening. Uncle Peter still didn't agree that his employee had taken time off for that reason, but he was amused by their audacity.

Laurie still had a hard time concentrating. While the others were talking, Laurie's ideas went elsewhere as she looked up at the mountain. A moment later, she found herself alone with Uncle Peter. Brandon had joined Angela in the house because he wanted to confide with her about Laurie and her recent behavior. He confessed to Angela, "The other night, she massaged me fiercely and told me she thought I was dying. Yesterday at the demonstration she was circling around me, it was so weird. This morning she was talking to herself in front of the mirror."

Outside, Laurie and Peter talked about work. He told her that Fernand, a driver of the family company, had checked into the hospital last night. Laurie gasped with concern. Something was wrong. "What happened to him? He sounded good yesterday morning!" While Peter explained the situation, Laurie was confused stepping back and forth between other realities: this one and the one from Brandon's novel story. Because Fernand had participated in the two-minute trailer that promoted Brandon's novel, she thought it was the reason for his hospitalization. He had played the role of a priest who was chased by evil, and weirdly she associated the sudden hospitalization with the possibility that the evil touched him. *Evil probably found him and now Fernand's body feels discomfort!*

"I will try to go and see him at the hospital," she told Peter with a small panic in her eyes. "I'm sorry again for the mistake I made yesterday. I don't know what is happening to me. I can't concentrate like I usually do!"

To reassure his niece, Peter said, "I'm sure you'll get over it." He gave her a couple of comforting pats on her shoulder.

His simple act of kindness activated Laurie's idea on another topic.

"Do you know we have the same astrologic Chinese sign?"

Her words went faster than her thoughts again. While Peter was answering that his sign was the Dragon, Laurie was thinking, *Why have I said that?* Nevertheless, she continued, "I know. Mine too. Your element is water and mine is fire."

Peter smiled. Laurie shared that she spent some time lately reading up on Chinese signs. She explained where her interest in this subject originated.

"About three years ago, I saw a dragon behind my back."

Peter was doubtful. Laurie explained she saw the dragon during a session with Mrs. Hélène, a spiritual lady who believes in healing mental and physical illness with herbs, or by cleaning their etheric body, than with pills. Peter seemed to have a vague idea of what Laurie was talking about.

"The lady was explaining to me the difference between spirit and soul, physical body, and etheric body. I was aware of each part of my body when suddenly, I saw an image like a hologram of a dragon appearing behind my back. I saw him in the corner of my left eye. I wasn't afraid. I was staring at the vision, waiting to know what the dragon wanted. Besides breathing and blinking a couple of times, he wasn't moving much. He seemed to be listening to Mrs. Hélène and me. Because he was leaning on my back, it felt like it was a part of me but somewhere else billions of miles away, and billions of years ago."

Laurie didn't have any filters anymore, and it was the first time she had said that much detail to anyone other than Miguel and Brandon.

"When the dragon finally disappeared, I told Mrs. Hélène about it. She said she had not seen it, but she had felt a presence and asked it to leave me. She told me I had probably seen that entity in my etheric body, and this was a place belonging to the fourth and fifth dimension. It's hard to explain, but in that dimension, time doesn't exist.

Peter was listening and Laurie concluded, "I never saw him again, but since then, I've been very interested in the stars, the Chinese signs and everything around us. I am convinced that there are many more things around us than the things we are able to see."

Peter took a different position and said, "I am concerned about what is happening to you Laurie."

Laurie didn't understand what he meant, as Peter continued, he asked his niece if she had taken any drugs.

"Of course not!" was her quick answer. "Why are you asking me that?"

Peter simply responded, "Because it is the only reason, I find plausible in relation to your new way of acting and thinking. I'm thinking that in the last few days you might have used hallucinogenic drugs..."

Amused, she responded, "Maybe I hallucinated for no reason, but I think I'm sensitive/receptive to natural phenomena."

Still in his thoughts, Peter seemed to reflect on the matter.

"You remind me of your mother. She really liked those kinds of subjects... numerology, astrology, cosmic science. I loved talking to her."

As she heard those lovely words, Laurie was fulfilled. She asked if she could have a moment to relax. As she walked towards the pond, she remembered the vision in the morning of Jesus in front of water.

She turned back at Peter and proclaimed, "You have a big and beautiful lot filled with underground water!" She smiled and added with confidence, "I believe this land is sacred and has been blessed."

It was noon. Laurie was standing next to the first pond, admiring the surrounding area, and taking deep breaths. She silently thanked Tim for guiding her to a pond. She found the perfect place, and confident, with her arms and hands open to welcome all the happiness she could receive into her being. She felt strong with both her feet well planted into the lawn while standing straight up and breathing clean fresh air. Everything seemed to be perfect while she looked at her favorite church in the distance on Mirabaska Mountain, where her maternal grandparents, their stillbirth baby, and Hetty, her mother, were buried.

After a peaceful moment, she walked to join Brandon, Angela and Peter. She realized that she wanted to jump, laugh, and spin around, dancing like a happy little girl because she felt joyful. But at the same time, she felt she had to hold back those strong feelings, otherwise, if other people saw her, they might think that she had lost her mind. She wanted to express her overload of happiness, but the reality of how society usually puts a bad name on someone who's different resurfaced.

Annoyed by this judgment, she denied herself from feeling free. It was with great melancholy that she repressed her happiness and walked on. She asked the universe, *Why should we stop ourselves from feeling free? Especially when it doesn't hurt anyone! Who chooses what we can do or cannot do and why? Since when? Can the mentality change?*

Like a magnet, she was attracting the truths from Heaven. Her questions were answered through a mixture of feelings, thoughts and reappearing memories from past lives. She saw the history from the beginning of civilization. Particularly, why we failed at finding our freedom and harmony, and deeper on another level, God versus the Devil was almost tangible.

Laurie had to slow down her thoughts in order to try to comprehend what was going on. She saw an image of a snake which was trying to communicate something to her, but she couldn't understand the message it was trying to convey. She just knew it was trying to corrupt and misguide her. Strangely, she had the feeling that the snake didn't know that she was observing ITS behavior. Laurie witnessed the ways the snake had done so much harm to humanity; the serpent seemed to constantly be hiding itself behind a foggy, grey substance and injecting bad thoughts directly into the minds of individuals. Laurie was amazed at that vision because she was seeing it without fear as she was surrounded by pure white light. Amazingly she understood that something bigger was protecting her and showing her how evil had acted in the minds of leaders throughout history.

On the drive back home, Brandon was quiet. On the contrary, Laurie was speaking fast trying to share with him the instances she received from the Universe. She had no filter and didn't hold back on the strong message she thought she had received, in a natural way, and thought it was her answers on why she couldn't feel free.

Brandon was driving the car, Laurie grimaced, expressing disgust while mentioning a few greedy scumbags who wanted to hang on to power and control, who had crucified Jesus because they were afraid and didn't understand His abilities. Later in time, others had called healers "witches." They had chased away the healers, those who were working in harmony with the earth, and literally burned them at the stake, presumably to rid them of imaged curses, because they didn't understand their gifts of healing. "They were healing people with garnishes from the earth and they were simply open-minded!"

With a vague idea of mental illness, Laurie got closer to Brandon. "Isn't this the same for those who are diagnosed with a mental disorder? We isolate them, drug them, and get them out of society because those in position of power, don't understand that others can see things they don't!"

Laurie leaned comfortably into her seat and continued talking about the way some leaders throughout history had been manipulated by evil; some kings who had encouraged slavery, some priests who had lied, hide and manipulated the first biblical text to keep the true intention of God for us. Other priests who also had used their power and committed sexual abuse, which caused most people to turn their backs on the church, and some politicians who overtaxed, leaving only a few to grow financially and morally.

Laurie didn't stop talking, which was unusual. Even as they climbed the stairs to their apartment, she stopped and made sure that Brandon looked at her. She lowered her voice and said, "Those leaders had been easy prey for the devil. Think about it—where is the easiest place to instigate discord? It's on the top level!"

"Lo, what do you want to eat?" Brandon said, casually switching topics.

"I don't know; I'm not hungry. I'm not feeling well. I've got a lot of ideas in my head."

Without bothering to look at her, he said, "You should write. It would be good for you. I'm going to make spaghetti."

"Thank you, writing is a good idea. I have so many ideas to help humanity."

Laurie didn't even take the time to sit down as she placed papers and pencils on the table. She leaned over to write quickly so as not to forget all these precious ideas swirling around in her head. She was upset thinking about the persecutors over history. She found them weak for allowing themselves to be manipulated by the devil and directed to do such harm to humanity. But then she sensed someone was telling her, "How can you judge? You don't know how long and how much they might have fought against it—against using their authority to commit those manipulations."

"Right!" Laurie felt like it was so simple to understand. *We shouldn't be angry at each other but be aware of the devil's manipulation. How could it be taught again?* She wondered.

"Laurie, dinner is ready. Are you going to stop writing for a moment?" Brandon said as he grabbed bowls from the cabinet.

Laurie didn't realize it, but her sweetheart was frustrated and concerned about her situation. She sat with him to eat, but her mind was elsewhere. She didn't want to lose track of her thoughts so, in between bites, she went back to the counter to add notes.

Dissatisfied with her weird actions, Brandon asked her what she was doing. Normally, she would have been aware that her activities were inappropriate.

"I am writing down the names of the delegates that I had seen in the last newscast," she answered in haste, because in an amazing way, she felt that with her new powerful abilities, she was able to identify which candidates were surrounded by white and pure light, or by foggy, grey smoke. The latter meant the candidates were fighting against evil and needed to be helped.

Brandon grumbled indiscernible words. Before he went out on the balcony, she apologized, "Sorry, it's going too fast in my mind. I don't have time to explain to you."

She continued to write, unaware that Brandon was calling a friend who works with mentally challenged patients. He was uncertain about Laurie's behavior. He needed to know if her "automatic writing" (as he later called it) was a good or bad thing.

"Geneviève, this is Brandon. I need to talk to you. I don't know what is going on with Laurie. It looks like she's going crazy. She's been acting weird lately but today's the worst. She's talking about witches, kings, priests, evil, and now she's writing like crazy, about politics, I think."

"I'm sorry to hear that." Geneviève added, "The only advice I can give you is to pay attention if she tries to hurt herself or others. In that case you should call the police and they will take her to the hospital. Otherwise, you can try to distract her with something else."

Brandon thanked Geneviève, hung up the phone and came back inside. Following Geneviève's advice, he tried a distraction and asked Laurie if she wanted to watch a movie.

"No thanks, I prefer to put my ideas on paper. I'm trying to free my mind a little bit more."

Brandon's anger finally got the best of him.

"I'm going to stop bringing you the newspapers every morning. You're too much of a politician and it's not good for you!"

Laurie did not respond to his comment, and Brandon walked away. Two ideas had just popped into her mind and created a new concept: politics and God's will. Laurie could see the weakness of humans through the devil's manipulation. She remembered Jesus had tried to teach humankind how to live together. She had heard people say that Jesus will come to help us. *Could that be the solution? Of course, Faith must be added as a principle for leadership. What's stopping us? Ego?* Laurie's head gestured to express her dissatisfaction about how history showed that religion doesn't balance well with politics. *But now that we know about the devil's manipulations, was it the reason why he interfered and brought discord between those two parties? Would humanity be better if we had followed Jesus's commandments? Would He have led us to freedom, evolving spiritually and supernaturally like the time traveling I experienced this morning? Could people believe now and choose Jesus as the leader of humanity? Is it possible to add a "Jesus" party to the two existing ones? Is it still possible or is it too late? Any solutions?*

She tried to calm down and pace the speed of the information that was passing through her brain in order to understand it. She felt somehow there were still solutions to return to God's path (no matter what each religion calls their Almighty, it referred to the One around and above us all with its light). Laurie's understanding was that every man had to be able to detect this Evil with his behavior and asked Mother Mary, like she once did, to find the strength to refuse it in his environment. Inwardly, Laurie was clapping her hands together and jumping for joy. *Yes, that's the solution!*

Brandon was watching TV, his back towards Laurie. She was still in the kitchen and tuned into the program he was watching. Impossible! Her vision was blurred when she looked towards the screen, but she didn't question what was happening. What she was seeing was a falsification of reality at that moment, and only assumed that her mind was preventing her from being distracted from the TV show.

Standing in the kitchen behind Brandon, Laurie began to turn in circles, her right index finger rested on her cheek. In a weird way, seeing herself in that position, thinking like a philosopher, her mind elevated to another level of wacky conjecture. While trying to understand what was going on, a funny thought emerged. She found herself in another epoch, seemingly out of her body. She could see herself among other philosophers—but she was in a man's body. The feeling of having already lived during the ancient time of men with long beards sitting around analyzing conspiracy theories of the time came to her.

She didn't have time to question if it was possible because she was already transported. Stunningly, she was sharing the confined space with about twenty other people dressed in beige tunics like herself. When she tried to take a closer look around the room and the people, the image faded and she could only hear the voices when they would speak. She couldn't see them anymore, but she knew they were still all together, and they had started to talk about the future. She heard some of them saying, "What would be best? What is likely to happen?" Everything seemed so real that this idea made her smile. *I've been a philosopher before! I've been a man before!* At no point during this time did she think she was disconnected from reality. In fact, she believed they were answering her question as to the possibility of a new political party being added. She continued with her inclinations with them about the "Faith Party," and she had a feeling of confidence that her fellow philosophers supported her.

In her physical form, Laurie was silent, but out loud deep inside her, she said confidently to the others, "Only to get there, we need the best leader humanity has ever seen. We need Jesus!"

Laurie heard the philosophers whispering. She felt their movements become a little more spirited. Their need to express themselves, to speak up was growing. She tried to hear what they were saying but they were speaking too quietly. Her desire to hear them was so compelling, her energy tempered their awareness, and they started to speak louder. One said, "Yes, it would be doable! On the other hand, people would oppose it because of their fears." Then another spoke with the trembling voice of old age, "Fear of the unknown... misunderstanding." Another, a younger voice, sure of his reply said, "Fear of change."

Many shared their thoughts, but no one objected, which led Laurie to persevere. "Okay, with faith we can change fears into great strength! How do we start the mission?"

No answer... Laurie waited a little longer... Nothing. A deafening silence engulfed the room. The precious time she had just shared with the philosophers was now gone. She couldn't hear them; she couldn't feel them either. In fact, she wasn't even thinking about them anymore. It was black, empty, nothingness. She remained in this state for a few moments, and then, little by little, another vision appeared. A whole new way of voting, which was much simpler and more honest was shown to her.

"Laurie, are you coming to bed?" Brandon asked, breaking through her vision.

"Not right now. I must put a plan on paper. I'll forget if I don't do it right now," Laurie replied hastily as she grabbed her pen and paper.

Brandon, unhappy, walked through the guest bedroom. Laurie dropped her pen and joined him.

"I'm going to join you soon after I'm done writing. I just thought of a new way of voting! We would need Victoria Blanchette (a famous TV show host) to explain the whole project to the nation and Mr. Smith (a prosperous businessman) for all his information systems and helicopters."

After giving her a facial expression that seemed to say, *I don't understand what you mean, and I don't care,* he shut the door of the guest room in her face. *Obviously, he doesn't want to sleep with me tonight!* Without making a big deal out of it, she went back to her drafts. She didn't feel offended, just found it sad that Brandon had to fall asleep with a sense of frustration in more ways than one.

While freely allowing these solutions to unfold so clearly and simply, another vision appeared: the entire population were gathering and were looking up to the sky. Some even had tears of joy streaming down their faces as they looked up to Heaven. As the collective emotions intensified, Laurie was attentive to the vision. She saw the light of many souls brightening as they had found their way back to faith.

Laurie was in a state of euphoria as she was writing down these thoughts on the sheets of notepaper, hoping she would remember the details later. Something she didn't have to care about was who the representative was going to be for the new party. It was her hope that if all the people were choosing the "Faith Party," then Jesus would appear. Seen by everyone, He would point out the right candidates, and with invisible directives, like intuition, they would know what to do to brings God's will into a governmental level and into the nation.

Tears of joy—but also of fatigue—flowed down her cheeks. Although Laurie still had a lot of ideas to transcribe, she was thinking of Brandon who would soon get up for work. She didn't want him to see her still writing. Exhausted but confident that this voting day would soon arrive, she put her pencil on her draft papers and quietly, she went to her room without ever second guessing the remarkable visions she had received that evening.

~ 6 ~

Meeting with her Inner Presence

Even though Laurie was exhausted mentally and physically from receiving an overload of information from above and beyond, she couldn't fall asleep. While lying on her bed, she realized she was no longer in control of her thoughts. That phenomenon was unusual to her, but she let herself be guided. She even felt a bit astonished at how the sensation seemed to suggest supernatural influences, pleasant and almost normal when her mind began to float in the air, and she was reminded of the trip she took with her best friend Arianne when they were younger.

They had crossed from east to west, throughout all of Canada. Laurie was revisiting and feeling the emotions again of when they had decided to go on a no-where-any-where trip without having a determined return date. She felt the intense emotion of happiness mixed with grief of saying goodbye to her friends and family. She still couldn't believe the courage they felt throughout the few obstacles they met along the way. Again, she experienced the feeling of awe and inspiration when, for the first time, they saw the immensely impressive wall at the beginning of the Canadienne Rocky Mountains.

But this time, Laurie was seeing them from above, like she was flying over the Rocky Mountains. She had a feeling of freedom while driving further west among those majestic mountains, and relief when they had finally decided to settle in a beautiful village an hour north from Vancouver. She saw herself again with Arianne, with a feeling of joy while jumping and dancing when they knew they could stay in that peaceful village named Whistler. It was the same day they both found jobs before running out of money. They shared a sense of pride while learning to snowboard, enjoying the thrill of riding down the endless, generously laden snow powdered hills. What an intense emotion she felt when after many months she had returned home, not announced, surprising and hugging each of her family members and friends.

The avalanche of emotions was so strong that she allowed them to be expressed while crying in her pillow to avoid waking up and alarming Brandon.

Smiling, she was grateful for living that marvelous adventure once more, in an incredible way. As she lay in a more comfortable position in her bed, she noticed Brandon was getting ready for work in the next room. Her mind was still floating in the air and somehow, it seemed to her that some kind of Energy was now next to her trying to guide her, to help her understand what had happened. The discomfort in her body was growing like a constant quivering in her stomach and in her throat. She felt that she was back at the time when she returned from her trip, living in the downstairs room of her parents' house and back in the office working for her aunt and her uncle. The feeling of sadness and impatience had taken over again. At that time, Laurie had prayed for guidance and after a good talk with her friend Anne, Laurie had decided, for a second time, to quit everything again, to follow her desires and go see what the world had to offer. Following that decision, Laurie's discomfort had faded, and a delightful feeling of lightness had taken place. It was a feeling of freedom that she could appreciate again. When she was finally ready to travel and see the world; she felt no fear about the future that awaited her. Instead, she had this deep sense of self-confidence. Even though she was traveling alone on this new journey, unconsciously she never felt alone. In her bed, feeling astonished by this peace of mind, she remembered how peculiar but pleasant that feeling was at the time. *It was faith!*

Conscious, she heard the door of the apartment close, the sound of the keys locking the front door, the door of Brandon's van closing and finally the engine starting. He was going to work. She was disappointed because she hadn't gotten her goodnight kiss, but at the same time, she was relieved he didn't see her awake with teary eyes.

Laurie pulled her blanket up under her chin remembering her adventure. In the airplane, from one flight to another, she was going to Hawaii.

44

As she was about to land, a strange new sensation was now imposing itself on her. In the dark of her room, she felt the invisible Energy try to command her attention to the details and the meaning of the events that were about to come.

While she adjusted her position on the bed, preparing for the forthcoming experience, she saw herself waiting and getting her backpack at the baggage claim area of Honolulu airport. It was around 10 p.m., she felt happy and carefree while breathing the warm, moist air in the middle of the Pacific Ocean. She could see the palm trees outside, lulled by the wind. The salty scent of the ocean was spreading throughout that open-plain airport. She felt pure happiness until she realized the place was deserted. Laurie was just beginning to wonder where she was going to sleep...

The vision showed her when she was waiting in the area to get her huge backpack. Incredibly, a huge blue-white color ball of energy, but almost invisible, appeared, grew, and surrounded Laurie's physical body as she was putting her huge backpack on. With a more open understanding of the supernatural, she rose immediately from her pillow, happy like never before. Her mouth fully open trying to say something. The more she observed, the more it took the form of a higher Being; it was radiant, and it was two times Laurie's size. She was in admiration in front of this phenomenon. *I always thought I had a presence with me, but now I'm certain!*

Astonished, Laurie sat up in her bed with tears of happiness running down her face as she felt the energy surrounding her in the room. It was now content with her recognizing its presence. She also had a sense of contentment while believing in this phenomenon. Ready to know more about her previous adventure, she paid close attention to the continuing vision. The energy, the supreme Being, delicately pushed her to the information counter of the airport, taking her fears and reflections away. Laurie saw again the moment when she had talked with the lady who had said it would be difficult to find a place to sleep at this hour and during this busy time of the year.

A boy about Laurie's age had arrived and asked the lady where to get his rental car. He had heard the previous discussion and offered Laurie a ride to the youth accommodation in the nearby town where he had already booked a room for the night.

Remembering how lucky she had been that night, and throughout her trip, she had no more doubts she had been divinely guided. Fully grateful for the supreme Being's part in her life, Laurie cried even more out of joy for His help. She wondered, *Was it God? Was it my guardian angel?* Rather it was suggested that it was her inner presence, her superior Being. *Unbelievable! I just saw my soul's Energy!* Laurie was crying out of joy as she acknowledged she had a powerful force within her, or with her. Fortunately, Brandon was gone, and she could cry without embarrassment. She felt connected to her soul, and thanked this power sincerely for protecting her, helping her, and planning such an amazing trip.

On her first day in Hawaii, Laurie enjoyed the beach, the warmth of the sun, and the sound of the ocean. When her stomach growled, she tried to ignore it. With greater display, she remembered a strong powerful push telling her it was time to find a place to stay for the night. Laurie listened to the call. She picked up her heavy bag, gave it a boost and carried it on her back. Recalling this event, in the invisible next to her, Laurie sensed the happiness of the Being for her responding to His directive. She didn't procrastinate and went immediately to the first roadside, backpack overflowing on either side of her, thumb up, and had waited for someone friendly enough to drive her back to the hostel.

Back in her comfortable position, resting her head on her pillow, she remembered she had felt no stress, but rather a higher inner strength. She remembered feeling protected, and she had embraced this amazing feeling of freedom thinking it was the magic of this paradise island. *It was magic indeed. Because I had been guided!*

In her bed, Laurie was proud, happy, and amazed revisiting that adventure. She had been smiling at motorists for a few minutes when a red car stopped. A man with dark skin and a serious look had asked her where she was going, and how long she will be on the island. "I don't know, it depends if I can find a place to stay." Laurie had spoken faster than her thoughts. Without judging, the man told her he had been in that situation before. Laurie felt comfortable and safe immediately with him. Diego helped her find a place to stay, and he became Laurie's best friend on the island. He introduced her to his friends; most of them Mexican like him. He helped her improve her English, taught her some Spanish sentences, and always made sure she was doing fine. Diego was the reason why Laurie had been fortunate to stay almost six months in that wondrous paradise.

In this moment of plenitude, while thinking about her old friend, a feeling that he was related to the Maya Civilization came to her. She didn't pay too much attention to it as another vision had taken over. It was the day she met with another dear friend, Josh. They instantly became great friends, too. He was an American, a native of Saratoga, New York. He had a child's heart with respect for nature. They spent a lot of time surfing, driving around and exploring the island.

Hugging her pillow, she remembered the beauty of this place. She could see it again as if she was there, how perfectly generous nature was to this grandiose, pure, and heavenly tropical paradise—the vastness of the ocean, the sky so big and blanketed with the millions of stars shining in the infinite galaxy.

In a subtle but important way, her soul showed her another brief vision of an event that occurred a month prior, here in Quebec, in her apartment. Laurie revisited when she had opened the door and welcomed two young men: an American and a Mexican.

It was during the afternoon, and Brandon was upstairs in the room working on his computer. They knocked on her door and surprisingly, Laurie had welcomed those strangers inside before she even knew the reason for their visit. Their appearance and their way of speaking reminded her of her two good friends from Hawaii—Diego and Josh.

The strangers had explained that they were visiting Quebec, and they wanted to talk about Jesus, saying He was still alive. Laurie had listened to them with respect since she had always liked hearing about Christ. Both young men had difficulty speaking French as it was their second or third language. One spoke more and seemed to be thirsty. So, Laurie had offered each of them a glass of water, which they greatly appreciated. Recanting the memory of when she envisioned giving them the glasses of water, Laurie's head suddenly turned to the right. It was as if in the invisible, something had thrown a net into her subconscious and captured her thoughts. *What am I supposed to understand? Why are you reminding me of those moments?*

The image became more clear. The boys had told her, "Jesus is still alive. We and our congregation believe that He's here in Quebec." Abruptly, a new scene during their conversation appeared. The two boys were both staring at Laurie, trying to convince her that she was Him. They were not allowed to say it, but mind to mind, they were telling her, *Don't you know it? You are Jesus!*

Without moving in her bed, Laurie was shocked. Her mouth and her eyes were both wide open as she couldn't believe this story. She immediately pushed that idea away. *This is ridiculous!*

It was around four o'clock in the morning, with tears in her eyes and exhausted, Laurie was begging to sleep. But the Energy next to her quickly reminded her about another serious event: the "millennium bug." Her journey in Hawaii was during the end of the nineties when calendars were about to turn to the year two thousand. Most newscasts had distressed the population by saying that computers could stop working properly if the machines didn't recognize the date 2000. The media stated it could be devastating for the economy and all data and files stored in all computers, including government mega systems, could be lost forever. While remembering when she had heard about the "computer bug," the Energy seemed to suggest to her that she hide away during that event; just like Jesus had to hide.

Incredulous and unsure to fully understand, Laurie grabbed her pillow, rearranged her body, and turned to the side trying to physically avoid that subject. She couldn't allow her mind to believe she was like Jesus. She ended up thinking she had been guided to move away because she would have been so stressed at her work, which was mostly spent on a computer.

Laurie tried to settle down comfortably, surrounded by pillows to comfort herself. She closed her eyes and wished for a peaceful night. She took many deep breaths trying to control her brain. Her mind enabled the thoughts of Jesus to dissolve on their own while her mind had begun to fly again. Laurie was revisiting a trip she went on with another friend: They had crossed the United States from New York to California and stayed a few days in Santa Barbara on the west coast. From there she thought she could continue flying to Hawaii, but she preferred to be guided. She had no resistance, no fear, no questioning. She felt light and free. Always guided by the Energy, flying her way back home over the many states she had visited, she heard a little inner voice whispering, *I've been here, and I've been there*. It was like the Energy was smiling at her, waiting for her to realize the incredible phenomenon. While Laurie was wondering what it could be, she heard, "Look, you can fly!"

That thought made Laurie laugh and scream at the same time. The funny part was she was seeing herself make presidential-style speeches all over Canada and the United States. The scary part was that within the depths of her awareness, her reasoning about the outlandish episodes caused her to think she was going crazy.

Because it was too much, she got up from her bed and abandoned trying to sleep. *Another sleepless night, I guess! I better leave before Brandon comes back from work.* Quickly, she got dressed, left a note on the table informing Brandon that she had gone for a walk before going to work, and rushed to leave before he returned from his night work.

~ 7 ~

Fourth Anniversary of her Mother's Death

Monday morning, May 14, 2012

The sun was rising. Laurie had not slept for three days and wasn't questioning what was happening. She felt tired and she was looking forward to finding a way to regain some strength and replenish her energy before starting her work week. She realized that it would help her to return and spend some time at her uncle's property, next to the pond. Because it was so early in the morning and she was so close to her aunt and uncle, she didn't call them to ask for their permission and soon arrived, unusually unannounced.

She quickly settled by the pond and began taking deep, calming breaths. She admired the view towards the church and the cross on the mountain in the distance across open fields in front of her. Today was exactly four years to the date her mother had passed away, but Laurie had not remembered it yet. She was trying to relax but felt ashamed and preferred to leave this resting place and be an hour early for work; later explaining her presence there to Angela and Peter.

In the meantime, Brandon arrived home and read Laurie's note, which worried him. He needed to talk but couldn't think of anyone to call at this early hour. He tried to fall asleep but couldn't.

Exiting the property's yard, and preparing to turn right like she usually does, Laurie's internal instinct told her to take a left instead. Since meeting with her inner presence last night, Laurie was even more attuned to listening to her intuitions. She waited for a moment at the edge of the road to try and understand. *Why turn to the left?* Nothing! There was no answer! She finally decided to turn left because in the end, both ways take about the same amount of time to get to her job.

Laurie's heart began to beat with joy when she saw that not much further ahead was the bell of Mirabaska Church, and quickly realized this road was bringing her straight to her mom. She was amazed how that turnabout ended up happening. *Why didn't I think about it before!* Grateful, she thanked her guide. *I'm going to spend this free time with my mother before going to work.*

While driving toward the church, Laurie was enchanted by this idea. The early morning sky was already clear. She was pleased with the weather and had a feeling that something special would happen today. She felt her mother's spirit was waiting to see her. Indeed, Hetty appeared as an illusion in the sky. Laurie was seeing her mother with a gleaming smile on her etheric body. Her blond hair was slowly moving in the air. She was wearing a white tank top and three quarter length jeans similar to what she wore in her physical life. She was beautiful!

Through the vision, Laurie's mother was looking at her from above, smiling, clapping her hands together as she leaned forward trying to kiss her daughter. Laurie could feel her mom's joy and excitement because her daughter was seeing her. When the vision disappeared, Laurie felt pampered to have had this chance to share another special moment with her mom; despite their two different worlds.

As Laurie walked to her mom's grave, a huge smile stretched across her face. She wondered if she should tell a loved one about this supernatural moment she had just experienced with her mom. In 2012, she didn't think many people could understand. She welcomed this experience, *Mom, that contact we just shared will be in my heart and memory forever. We can be proud of ourselves.*

Once arriving at the cemetery, Laurie walked to the first aisle on the left that would lead her to her mother's grave. She was simply and completely content to be living in this present moment. She looked up a little as she was about to climb the small slope. It seemed a bit strange but also pleasant when the deceased from above their tombs started to greet her! She could sense some kind of energy hovering above their stones. She greeted them with a nod and mentally said hello. She became excited and exclaimed silently, *All those times that I've been here, this is the first time I understand this phenomenon! It's all connected!* She was amazed at how this accumulation of souls had just revealed themselves! She could feel them! Interact with them! She was experiencing an exceptional, though surreal, moment in time!

She continued to walk slowly and along the way, she took the time to read the names written on each headstone. It seemed to help her connect with the energy of the soul that was entombed in each grave. She heard whispering. They were talking to her! They wanted to express their voices.

Then...

An invisible force struck Laurie head-on at the height of her chest. It tilted her head backwards as she forcibly let out a breath of air... allowing her to welcome her new reality. Because she was able to see them and hear them, the souls were asking her to help humanity! Wishing for a better understanding, Laurie asked them, *How can you know that this is what I wish, helping humanity?* She stopped in the middle of the aisle and added, *Why can I hear you? Why can I feel your presence?* She felt a force or an energy a few centimeters from her right ear saying, "During your life on earth, we have seen you with ... Julie ... Catherine ..." As she heard names scrolling, she saw the image of an old lady. Even though she had seen her only once before, Laurie assumed that Energy belonged to her childhood friend, Julie's grandmother.

Laurie appreciated this supernatural phenomenon that was allowing her to be in contact with another world on the other side of the veil. It was as if all spirits floating around were the energy of souls connected with this association of expired former earthly citizenry of her town.

During this phenomenon, she heard a powerfully persuasive voice exalting, "We believe you have a pure soul!" Then another softer and wiser voice added, "Of course, there have been a few faults, but your way of seeing your mistakes, accepting them, and making sure they do not happen again is proof of great wisdom." Another, with a friendly and sincere voice said, "For millennia, Laurie, you have been trying to be and do good, you believe in a better world. In this life, you have chosen to be born under the sign of Libra, which tells us that you have chosen justice and equality. Since you were a little girl, your soul has chosen and placed good people around you to help you in your journey. You have learned to listen, you have opened up to life, you have faith in something greater than yourself! You've learned to make pride your ally. You have the good of others at heart." Then the voice went on, "This is your answer. You managed to follow your guide by coming here today, and that's why you can hear us!"

Standing tall in the aisle of the cemetery, Laurie had no words to define the joy she felt when hearing those wonderful compliments coming from the ethereal kingdom above! The exchange seemed so real to her that while slowly walking, she had to put her hand in front of her mouth and nose to mute her cries of delight. She was grateful and amazed to hear these compliments. At no time had she ever wondered if she was hallucinating or disoriented—except perhaps when she remembered she had walked around almost every path of the cemetery, nodding to let the deceased souls know that she accepted the mission, "But to succeed, I will need your help and strength."

As she left the church parking lot, shy but happy, she looked up at the sky thinking, *Is this possible?*

The short drive to her job went well. Laurie took a deep breath as she got out of her car, took a second deep breath to contemplate and greet nature. The sky was perfectly blue, and the air of spring smelled perfectly fresh. While looking at Mount Mirabaska, she admired the cross at the top and the new lookout point structure that had been built not too long ago. It was a perfect place to stand and admire the regions around. While stretching, she admired that new structure created by man, in perfect harmony with nature.

Laurie entered the building and then unlocked the door of her office. Once she walked in, she didn't feel the same way as she usually does—she didn't like this strange feeling! *This place is too small, too stuffy, and too gray!* Without any windows of a direct view to the outside, this space felt restricted. Putting down her purse and keys, she breathed deeply as she needed it. She felt like she was choking; as if an intense, vibrating ball was stuck between her lungs. She breathed again to help free herself... then something happened, like when your ears are blocked, and suddenly— poof— you hear better. She wasn't sure what had just happened, but it seemed that she had a sense of expansion—as if her etheric body had gained some space.

Laurie called her boss as usual to verify that he had instructions she needed for the dispatching part of her job.

Peter answered, "No, there has been nothing yet. Did you come home this morning?"

"Yes, sorry. I didn't want to disturb you."

Laurie's voice was shaking a little, and she realized her entire body was shaking as well.

"There are no problems. You can come by whenever you want. We'll talk later!" Peter remarked.

Laurie couldn't concentrate, even on the usually simple tasks. She was looking at the phone, waiting for it to ring while spinning her computer's mouse on the mouse pad. The idea of calling Mrs. Victoria Blanchette and Mr. Smith came to her mind. Laurie wasn't thinking realistically.

She looked on the internet at Mrs. Blanchette's company website and quickly found the phone number of the TV host. She deliberated for a few minutes to find the right words to share the new concept of voting for the upcoming election that she had envisioned last night. Laurie could hardly believe this was about to happen. *Wow, I'm going to talk to Mrs. Victoria and then with Mr. Smith.* Despite feeling a little bit of stress when the phone rang, Laurie wondered if they also heard the deceased talking this morning or the philosopher last night.

No receptionist answered. Laurie left a message on the answering ma- chine to return her call. *Thank goodness!* Because she wasn't feeling effective at the moment. Her body continued trembling and for the first time, her right hand didn't want to respond. In fact, her whole right arm was heavy. She had trouble getting her thumb and index finger to pinch together. She had to concentrate a lot to hold her pencil between her fingers and it was even harder for her hand to write legibly. Laurie wasn't feeling well physically. Morally, however, she was ready to try again and make the call. Because she was feeling trapped inside and needed more space, she went outside and called, using her cell phone. This time, the receptionist answered and said Mrs. Victoria was not available and asked if she was waiting for her call. "No, but she will be very pleased to hear what it is about." Laurie said confidently. The receptionist took Laurie's contact information thinking she had heard this before. As Laurie hung up, she wondered where she found this courage of calling and encouraged herself, *This is what I had to do!*

When she reentered the office, Laurie came close to collapsing. It was probably due to lack of sleep, resulting in a loss of energy. Or maybe it was because she was desperate? But gratefully an idea came to her. She called Aunt Angela and asked her, for the first time, if she could invite herself to lunch with them at their house. She needed help, comfort, and food. It would also allow her to be closer to her boss, and Uncle Peter could see that she might not be able to finish her workday.

"Of course, you can come have lunch with us. I made fish and mashed potatoes," Angela said.

The image of that meal was already bringing her appetite back. Despite feeling a little relief, Laurie felt emotionally drained and exhausted.

"Thank you so much Angela! I will see you soon!"

~ 8 ~

Lightning Rod Phenomenon

Alone in her car while driving to her aunt's house, Laurie was experiencing, for the very first time in her life, the most bizarre feeling that her body had ever had. Inside her, there was a river of energy moving as if it wanted to flow outward. When she realized that there was a dam blocking the flow of good breathing at the height of her chest and causing her pain, Laurie's head immediately was thrown backwards. Fortunately, she still managed to keep her eyes on the road. In a rush, she leaned her face near the half open window on the driver's side to take advantage of the refreshing trade winds, hoping to feel better by letting the energy out. Her mouth and throat opened to bellow out a deep, powerful, hollow, and intriguing sound that came from the depths of her guts. Tears were gushing. She was not only surprised and intrigued—she was worried.

But the more she let out the roars, the better she felt. Tears of fatigue were uncontrollably streaming down her cheeks until she arrived at her aunt's house.

Angela came outside to greet her goddaughter. She immediately noticed Laurie had been crying. In a maternal voice, she told her to go and relax while they waited for Uncle Peter to join them for lunch. She added with some doubt, "Come meet me when you are ready."

Laurie walked close to the same place she was in the morning. She had a hard time breathing because the dammed-up flow of energy was still within her. She didn't know what to do to free herself from it. She looked around, and even though her body felt uncomfortable, a feeling of happiness invaded her senses. She observed the impressive view of the pond beside her, the huge meadow between her and the mountain. Trampling on the lawn, trying to get the perfect view of the mountain, it was comforting to see the cross on the top and below, her favorite church, and the cemetery next to it. With both feet firmly pressed into the lawn and her head held high, her arms outstretched along her body and her hands open towards the mountain, her gaze fixated on the cross, and with all her heart, she begged the Lord to help her, and she prayed to Mother Mary to be by her side and protect her.

As she finished her prayer, it felt like something was happening under Laurie's feet. *Energy?* Her entire body began to tremble like when one is about to vomit. Her body felt uncomfortable; she was shaking and didn't know what was about to happen. Unencumbered tears welled up in her eyes. Aware of her condition, she was now ready to find out what was going to happen to her. She took a deep breath and... then suddenly, without holding anything back, she let it all out—a long piercing and painful whimper.

Angela was in the kitchen looking at Laurie from time to time. She became scared when she saw Laurie stepping on the grass and suddenly saw her head reflexively thrown backwards, and immediately began howling loudly. Angela panicked at the strange scene of her goddaughter, and the scary scream coming out of her niece. She didn't know what to do or who to call. She felt powerless.

From Laurie's point of view, the underground energy passed through her so strong that her head had no choice but to reflex backwards and at full blast, letting out a mighty howl. It was a mixture of power and sadness emanated out through the opening of her mouth to ascend to the heavens... Her body and mind had no resistance. Her arms moved on their own with the intensity of the energy that passed through her center core. It felt to her as if she was being used as a lightning rod, but from the earth to heaven.

It was noon. Laurie was looking directly toward the sun, with tears of discomfort streaming down the whole time. A few small white clouds became wispy as they rode through the incredibly huge, blue sky. Laurie couldn't stop the event (the energy stream) and didn't know how long it would take. Sounds vibrated intensely within her. The most rational idea that came to her then was that the earth was sending a message to the sun and to the entire Milky Way. She was afraid for a moment, as she imagined who this energy was trying to reach and why. *Aliens? Evil spirits?* But she immediately rejected this idea when images of good spirits, such as gods and angels, came to her.

She was aware that she was living this real moment. She also knew it was a strange experience! At the same time, in that position, she was wondering how that could be possible. Somehow, like a sixth sense, she understood that it was natural—as are lightning and tornadoes. *Nature is incredibly large and often incomprehensible!*

Still in action of sending piercing sounds straight up, seeming easy to reach deep into the outer worldly celestial spiritual home, Laurie felt like a wind of love and hope encapsulated her body and slowly calmed down the intensity of the screaming. And eventually, new sounds were transformed from powerful screams to sadness to something like cries of redemption. The vibrations began to resonate as if it was an old dialect. She thought this energy was in search of forgiveness and hope.

Then, the sounds emanating from Laurie's being became quieter, but clearer. She tried to interpret the ideas, emotions, sensations that were now travelling slower through her entire body. She wanted to know where those emotions were coming from. They sounded like incantations from another ancient anthem... expressed with perhaps the native Hebrew language. The chanting seemed to be from very old souls and dedicated to the heavens as a sign of gratitude.

Still in the same position with her head arched backwards, Laurie wasn't resisting any vibration or growling sounds that escaped from her mouth, even though she knew she was disturbing others. She thought of her aunt and uncle, *They must feel the need to call for help.* She thought of the neighbors, too, *Can they hear me?* With the hope of convincing herself, *No! I'm sure they can't! They live too far away to hear me!* Still doubtful, a vision appeared and seemed to be happening nearby. It was a deer which had just stopped and froze with one hoof in the air as if ready to run if needed. Immediately after, another vision of a hare which had suddenly stopped, appeared. Its long ears paid a lot of attention to its own surroundings. Same as the dear, it too, had kept one paw in the air, ready to make a quick exit. Both of their heads were held high, and their ears were moving as if they were listening to the same vibration as Laurie.

Even though she had undoubtedly terrorized her aunt and maybe the surrounding area, she finally enjoyed the moment. Even though it was weird, she felt privileged to have been part of this natural phenomenon—to have been a bridge of liberation between two worlds. She thought, *It was so powerful!* This experience had finally stopped, and she felt everything had been expressed. Laurie reclaimed her body, retreated from that spot, and sat a little further away on the lawn. Inwardly, she thanked Angela and Peter for allowing her to finish her accomplishment. *Maybe they didn't have a choice?*

Angela joined Laurie with arms folded across her chest. She seemed angry and told Laurie to never, ever do that again. *Unfortunately, I scared her. If I had witnessed such a scene, I would have been scared, too!* Angela then asked her to come inside.

While eating, Angela invited Laurie to spend the afternoon at her house and only take care of the phone calls. With a mix of gratitude and sadness in her look, Laurie nodded to confirm she accepted the invitation. Peter was looking at his goddaughter in a way he hadn't often done. All Laurie could say about her behavior and the screams was, "I don't know what just happened and why. But something similar happened in my car on my way here. I just felt like I had to let this all out! I feel better now."

Angela was still concerned, and Peter was thinking Laurie had consumed a lot of drugs which, of course, wasn't the case.

After a meal filled with emotion, they sat on the patio and enjoyed the beautiful spring day. While looking at the church, Laurie mentioned to them there had been no calls this morning. She found the situation very strange as she remembered, and shared, "It has been four years today my mom had passed away." Everyone went silent, and Angela remembered sadly that day when her sister had passed away.

Laurie reminded them what had happened a week later when they had buried her ashes, "Do you remember the four light rays that had appeared from heaven?" A special appearance had occurred in front of every one of Hetty's loved ones as they freed three doves as a sign of a new beginning for her. While they were all watching the doves fly in the sky returning to their homes, in the pure, blue, and cloudless sky, four rays of light had appeared from the heavens and shone on the four corners of the church. Everyone had been enchanted by the phenomenon. Some thought the phenomenon could be a passage for Hetty to go directly to heaven, others suggested it could be a ray for each member buried under the same tombstone; William the dad, Marie-Ange the mom, Hetty and Joseph, the stillborn brother.

Peter remembered sadly he had not been able to attend the burial because it was too busy at work that day. Angela remembered how intriguing that moment had been, "Yes, I remember the four rays." Laurie wondered if the four rays of light meant that in four years, another supernatural phenomenon will happen, exactly what she just experienced an hour ago; a bridge between the earth and the sky would be created.

***

Four years prior. May 2008. Laurie's parents had been divorced for a while already. Hetty had been hospitalized and she asked her two children to come and meet the doctor. Together, they had learned Hetty had cancer, and unfortunately it already spread throughout her body. Because she was already terminally ill, Hetty didn't want to receive treatment, with the intention to live her last weeks out of a hospital room.

It seemed like only a few days later, Hetty was lying on a hospital bed, at her best friend's apartment. Some nurses were coming about two times per day, and a schedule of availability had been created for Hetty's loved ones to take turns caring for her. It was comforting to Laurie to see her aunts and her mother's longtime friend spending time with her mom.

Laurie's first turn was during an evening. In the only room of the apartment, Hetty was lying down on a hospital bed, and wasn't talking much. But she listened silently to all Laurie's sorrows for being such a self-ish daughter, mostly during her teen period. Hetty tenderly held her daughter's hand and smiled at her while saying everything had been perfect to her. She then asked to rest a little.

Hetty had left a small book on the nightstand near the bed. She knew Laurie was curious and would look at it. Indeed, Laurie read the title on the book cover: *Science Cosmic, the Laws of Attraction.* For a moment, Laurie was a bit surprised that her mother's last reading would be this kind of literature. She quickly grabbed the book while remembering her mom used to take cosmic science and numerology classes a long time ago. Sitting on the bed next to her mother, Laurie didn't take the time to get comfortable.

The nightlight in the room gave her just enough light to read the first chapter; the seven laws of attraction and look carefully at every detail of the illustration. It was a picture of a human body encircled with arms extended. There were lines drawn in triangles and numbers, and the names of the 7 chakras. Laurie was turning the pages slowly, trying to understand the laws by looking attentively at each image when suddenly, in an unexpected way, the entire ambiance of the room changed. She felt as if she was out of her body. Everything seemed to be so deep. She took a moment to analyze this strange but pleasant feeling. She was calm, feeling at peace even though she knew she was about to lose her mom. In that feeling of freedom, neither time nor physicality mattered. It was like her mom's soul and hers were hanging in the center of the universe and still, they were so close to each other.

Without knowing, in 2008, it had been Laurie's second out of body experience. She questioned herself on what was happening and suddenly, all this feeling of grandeur faded away. Her mom released a soft breath and put her hand on her daughter's thigh. In doubt, Laurie looked at her mother. Without saying a word, Hetty smiled at her daughter seeming to tell her that she also felt the special moment they just experienced. Hetty had closed her eyes and Laurie returned to her reading with a sense that she was surrounded by love and a strong feeling that her mom just shared with her all her studies and knowledge about cosmology science. Or, was this phenomenon about Hetty helping and preparing her daughter to let her go? This feeling of deepness had been a special event to Laurie.

The very next day, Laurie had just went to bed, and her phone rang. It was 10 p.m. Afraid to hear any unwanted news, she took a moment before answering. It was her aunt Angela, and in a calm voice she said, "Laurie, if you want to say a last word to your mom, it's time for you to come."

Laurie cried as she said, "Yes, I'm coming." She cried as she got dressed, as she drove, and even more when she arrived and she saw her mom in a coma. Appreciatively though, the room was already warm with the presence of her brother and some aunts and uncles. In order to help her calm down, her mom's older sister, Aunt Georgia mentioned to Laurie in a warm tone while pointing to the sky, "You know Laurie, here we are sad that your mom is about to pass away, but in Heaven, other family members and friends are joyful, and it is with great anticipation that they await her coming." When she heard her sensible words, for a moment, she had a sensation of her grandparents' presence and as soon as she noticed that feeling, they appeared to her like a vision. From above, at the ceiling height, they were both looking down with tenderness at their daughter, with a smile on their etheric faces. Peacefully, they were waiting for Hetty to pass and come to them. Laurie strongly hugged her Aunt Georgia, as if she was hugging her dear grandparents.

A nurse who arrived to verify Hetty's physical state had explained to everyone in the room that Hetty's body will probably have reactions before passing, and it only means that the body needs more morphine. She added it was a normal reaction and the patient doesn't feel any pain. She then advised Laurie, "You can tell your mom you are ready. It will help her go." Laurie was standing on the left side of her mom's bed, and Patrick, her brother, was on the right side while aunts and uncles were taking turns at the foot of the bed.

About two hours later, Hetty's body reacted in a way Laurie and Patrick had never seen before. For a few seconds, Hetty's body would raise from the pillow, like she would be trying to say something but, without saying anything she would return in her lying position. Laurie couldn't see her mother's face since she was on the other side. As the nurse suggested, Laurie was telling her mom while caressing her arm, "Everything is going to be fine, Mom. We are ready, you can go." But during those moments, Patrick seemed to be scared or sad. He was shouting, "Something is wrong. She is not okay." Their aunts were trying to calm him down while showing him how to put some water on her lips to refresh her. After a few of that same kind of episodes, Laurie sat next to her brother. Her mom's body had another spasm, and it was the first time that Laurie saw her mom's face during a contraction. Hetty's dying body raised again for a few seconds, her lips were tight together, and her eyes were open. Laurie was shocked to see her mom's two eyes looking in two different directions: one at her children, and the other at her siblings.

Laurie took a deep breath searching for courage before caressing her dear mom, and telling her again, "It's okay mom, you can go. We are ready to let you go even if we are going to miss you." Hetty returned to her calm position and still holding her hand, amazed with her mom's new look of outward turning of eyes, Laurie added, "Everything is going to be fine." But what a surprise when Hetty's etheric body impulsively sat straight up in bed and shouted, "I am ready, but how do I leave my body?" Only Laurie had witnessed this phenomenon. During one last breath, she saw her mother's etheric body returning down into her physical body and disappeared. Stunned, she looked around and her surprising emotion took over—no one seemed to have noticed anything since their expressions were still neutral. Laurie suddenly realized her mom had just asked for help.

Tears began to stream down Laurie's cheeks as she started thinking how she could help her mom. For the first time she wondered, *How would I leave my body if it was me in that situation?* She closed her eyes. "Mom," she said silently after taking a long deep breath. "If it was me, I think I would take the time to look at the people around me." Laurie took another deeper breath as she felt her mom was listening. "I would tell them I love them. And then I would tell them goodbye." As Laurie took another breath, she felt her mom was following her breathing. She continued, "I would close my eyes and I would wait for my loved ones from the other side to come pick me up." A few seconds later, Laurie cried even more as she heard her mother's last breath. She heard the others in the room whispering at each other sharing they were thinking it was her last breath.

Laurie kept her eyes closed to accompany her mom until she was sure she had passed to the other side and reached her parents. Astonishingly, Laurie sensed the surprising emotions of her mother when she saw herself detached from her body. Then she saw Hetty smiling at her parents as she met them. Then she saw Hetty's peaceful emotion when she looked at her daughter Laurie and told her tenderly from above, "Goodbye my dear precious daughter." The images of Hetty, and her emotions had disappeared. Back with her own emotions mixed with sadness and happiness for her mother, Laurie took another deep breath, wishing the best for her dear mother. When she opened her eyes, she felt grateful and relieved to notice the peaceful look on the inanimate face Hetty left behind.

Since the death of her mom, Laurie truly believes in the continuity of life, and thanked her mom for this most incredible gift she ever offered her—Laurie deeply felt that her mom had waited those long hours to have her daughter help her and experience the magic of a wonderful passing toward the other realm.

During the first year that had followed, there were a few times Laurie had visits from her mom. It was as if in between their two worlds, they were communicating as to forgive and understand why they had done things regarding specific events. Laurie appreciated deeply those moments when they were manifesting, but she wasn't running to it. She was only praying for her mother's soul to be protected and guided.

On the first anniversary of Hetty's death, Laurie visited her at her grave. As she was standing alone peacefully in front of her grandparents, Joseph, and her mother's tombstone, she had a vision. She saw her mother in the sky, in front of a master, seeming to be receiving confirmation that she had succeeded and was allowed to go into a higher level of spirituality. *Probably because during the last year, she had been able to be in contact with a mortal and have fixed things up!* Laurie thought as the vision continued.

Proud, the master was telling his student that her daughter on earth was observing her. In that particular moment, Hetty didn't seems sure what he meant, and her expression interpreted by Laurie was that her mother was detaching from her, and was going further in the Universe. But in that moment, Hetty didn't have the time to express her love to Laurie, who believed she was losing her mom for a second time... Sadly, Laurie had cried so much again, thinking she will never see her mom again. And because she couldn't explain to anyone that she was going through another grief.

~ 9 ~

Craziness or she Sees into Another Dimension?

Outside, everyone was seated on the patio, Laurie was telling Angela and Peter how strange it was that the business had not received any calls yet, since the morning. She suggested it could be related to the four rays of light that occurred, four years to the date that Hetty had passed away. As if by coincidence, Laurie's company cell phone finally rang. After a few calls in a row, Laurie sensed her mother was giving her reason for her thoughts, the time had stopped in order to realize it was a special day.

Unfortunately, in this reality, she was still having trouble concentrating over the phone and often had to ask the customer to repeat their words. Her hand wasn't responding. She couldn't write what she was hearing. In disbelief at what he was seeing, Uncle Peter finally jumped in and took the calls. Once the little rush was over, worried, Laurie told Peter, "Look at my shaking hand. I can't write; I can barely hold the pen!"

Slyly, Angela went inside and called Brandon to tell him of Laurie's new behavior. Outside, Peter calmed Laurie down, "Don't worry. These kind of things happen sometimes." Then he quickly changed the subject and oddly talked about politics. Laurie was surprised that her uncle talked about politics, therefore, she just remembered about the weekend protest.

Peter eventually left for work. Alone, Laurie was sitting comfortably on a rocking chair looking at the sky. At the sight of what she thought was an eagle, a crazy idea came into her reality; like in Brandon's book story, as the evil was lurking for the priest, now he was lurking for HER.

Laurie's cell phone rang and distracted her from her thoughts. It was Brandon. She noticed he was nervous because his voice was trembling slightly while asking her where she was, pretending he didn't know. "You know where I am," Laurie said impatiently. Changing subject, she told him she wasn't sure at what time she would be home. Remembering evil had lurked for Fernand, she had decided to go see him at the hospital.

Brandon couldn't hold it in anymore. Before hanging up quickly, he shouted, "Lo, I cannot take it anymore. I won't sleep here tonight. You are too weird!" Laurie hung up thinking it was just a bad moment. *He can wait. We'll talk later.*

Before leaving, Laurie thanked her aunt once again. She told her she was going to see Fernand at the hospital, and promised she would go to bed early to be in better shape for tomorrow.

***

While getting out of her car and walking towards the hospital, Laurie remembered how often she had come here. Her grandfather William had spent months hospitalized before passing away when she was a baby. And later her grandmother had also spent months hospitalized at the time when Laurie was a child, a teenager, and again when she was a young adult. Laurie was familiar with that hospital. She knew exactly where to go. Strangely, before entering the building, she focused on storing as much energy as possible in her being. She asked for help from above hoping she could heal Fernand.

Once inside, she felt like the atmosphere had changed. Her reality morphed into a deeper sense of awareness. She felt she could see through walls if she wanted to. She wasn't seeing from her eye's interpretation, but instead, the perception was coming from higher than herself—as if she had another head above hers. Without having to acknowledge the origin of this force, she felt stronger and more confident as she accepted the energetic charge that rained on her. She walked along the corridor with her head held high but in a nonchalant way. Laurie was taking her time to get a feel for the place, convinced she could cure all the sickness if only she could take the time to stop. But deep inside, she knew it was impossible so, instead, she internally prayed for their healing.

Laurie was a believer of energy manipulation and its power to heal a body from the inside out. But she felt an inner battle between hope and reason. At eye level appeared a white light, and in that bright light, she saw herself and many other healers applauding as they believed also in energy healing. But lower down, at the level of her stomach was a black image, and this force was trying to diminish her intended objective by telling her that it was a stupid idea. Laurie decided to not give the black image any importance. Without giving it a second thought, she chose the light and its powers.

As she walked to her destination, most people were looking at her. She smiled at them, and they revealed wonderful smiles in return. Shy, Laurie looked down at her feet. Emotionless, she saw sandals instead of the shoes she was supposed to be wearing. She saw herself walking differently and dressed differently. Laurie was not afraid of the crazy current innocent thoughts that were being manifested within her mental processes. Neither was she judging nor questioning seeing herself as if she was Jesus.

While still walking through the hospital hallways toward her destination, she simply accepted this implausible thought, and let it linger as if it were even a remote possibility. In a state of neutral emotion, she made eye contact with people. Therefore, she felt their expressions had changed, and interpreted their new looks as if they were able to see Him, Jesus through her. Through Laurie's imagination, they believed in Him! Laurie was hoping a miracle would happen so they would keep faith in Him.

She continued strolling along the corridor with absolute confidence. She was fearless and ready to heal, however, and whoever the Spirit in the Sky would direct her. Laurie was sincerely hoping for the best for humanity.

Fernand was happy to see Laurie. From his bed, he introduced her to his wife. The ladies shook hands. Denise sat back next to Fernand and Laurie stood at the foot of his bed. She turned to her co-worker and asked him what had happened. Fernand was saying it must be because of a virus in the water he had drunk. But unbelievably, Laurie saw a black and volatile spot near Fernand. Her understanding became even stronger; Fernand's discomfort was in fact the manipulation of evil. And this black spot was similar to the one that was invading her when she was younger. Like Mother Mary had done gracefully, internally, Laurie ordered this entity to leave and to never return. Remarkably, she saw the black and volatile spot move and finally disappear.

Laurie was amazed by her power. Proud, a little smile appeared on her lips while engaging in some friendly chit chat. But she remembered she had a mission to accomplish—heal Fernand! She asked for help from the world above. Laurie's facial expression began to change because she suddenly felt the energy flow to heaven. She believed her healing technique was working. It occurred to her that the souls in the cemetery (the ones she met during this morning's visit) were responsible for repealing the negative vibes. While continuing the chit chat, Laurie thanked the angels for their help. Then, there was nothing. She felt no more energy in the room and wondered what she was supposed to do. She stayed in the same position for a moment, only turning her head to Denise to continue the conversation. As she listened to Denise, a flood of love and energy began to descend from Heaven and spread throughout Fernand's body. Laurie smiled at Denise, turned to Fernand, and spontaneously asked him, "Did you feel anything wonderful in your body?" Fernand didn't understand what she meant. With confidence Laurie said, "I believe that a good energy is with you and that it will heal you."

Fernand laughed heartily and said, "I certainly intend to heal!"

Laurie was happy about his positivity. Gradually, she had no more feeling of supernatural effect, and she began to see again with her own physical eyes. Fernand thanked her for her visit saying it was very much appreciated. They held each other's hands and hoped to see each other again soon.

Laurie came out of the room with a few tears of joy streaming down freely, and a feeling of lightness, and grateful for the experience. The next afternoon, Fernand was discharged with no trace of any virus in his system. When she received that news, Laurie wondered if it was her work to be thankful for Fernand's recovery, or the medication, but she didn't receive any clue.

Brandon was in front of the TV when Laurie arrived home from the hospital. He didn't know what to say and said nothing. Laurie sat down next to him, snuggled up to him and held his hand which he responded well to. She felt like they were connecting emotionally. She just wanted to lean her head against his shoulder, watch the movie and think about nothing. Brandon wasn't sure anymore what was going on.

The movie had already begun, and the scene was taking place in a cave, or a bunker? The place seemed as if it had belonged to rare animals before but was now owned by a bunch of bad humans with their red eyes and their disgusting yellowish teeth, keeping warrior women as prisoners. The air in that underground place seemed almost impossible to be able to breathe in. Throughout the movie, Laurie felt she was witnessing another reality that was taking place in an epoch before, future, or maybe in another dimension.

Yet, Laurie was sure she was witnessing the battle between good and evil among the human eras. While paying close attention to the images, she shivered during a loud frightening noise. Laurie understood from this noise that huge stones had collapsed, and a door to the outside had finally opened. Most of the bad humans and the warrior women had quickly left behind that cold, damp and gloomy place. Strangely, once outside, it seemed they were now acutely aware of the sun as if they were seeing it for the first time. They were desperately breathing the pure air. And always in Laurie's understanding, the main tyrant strangely reminded her of her brother, and the main warrior woman strangely reminded her of her longtime good friend, Anne. Next to each other, while looking at the sun with admiration, their bodies seemed to be changing, and their aggressive behavior was calming down. Weirdly, Laurie felt she was about to witness a possible untold story of Adam and Eve.

The movie was ongoing when Laurie got up, happy with what she witnessed; there was no need to see more because she thought she knew the predictable eventual outcome.

"Wow! This movie is unbelievable! It was like the story of my brother and Anne! Have you seen it before?"

"No," Brandon said exasperated while Laurie didn't seem to care. Exhausted, she just wanted to go to bed and have a good night's sleep. Hesitant, Brandon asked her if she wanted him to sleep with her or in the guest room."

"Whatever you want, but I'd like you to sleep with me." Laurie said with a seduced look.

Only Brandon had fallen asleep when a surprising and loud noise was heard by everyone in the building, which shocked her. Laurie interpreted it as the same terrifying noise from the one-time opening door from the movie she just watched. *A door is opening to another world?* Terrified, Laurie was afraid to be brought to the terrifying bunker, where the battle of good and evil would take place. She immediately got up in a panic from the bed and exclaimed:

"They found me!"

"Who's that?"

"Evil spirits!"

"What?!"

Brandon didn't understand how scared Laurie was.

"What are you doing?"

Laurie was mumbling and talking to herself, trying to move fast. She picked up the brochures of the spiritual training she had taken and grabbed for the phone numbers of the people she trusted. *Tim, Lisa and Mrs. Hélène would probably know what to do if I disappear!*

Irrationally, Laurie had the crazy thought she was somehow Jesus and if something happened to her (to Jesus), that humankind could be in danger. "I must go to my uncle's property. I'm not safe here anymore!"

In a rush, Laurie put on the same clothes she had worn that day.

"Lo, I don't understand. Are you going crazy or what?"

Laurie turned to Brandon, "Did you hear that big noise? The big BOOM?"

"Yes..." he said and waited to know more.

"A secret door opened between this world and the bad world. They found me! I must go to Peter's place! I must take refuge in a holy area!"

Laurie spoke hurriedly. Brandon didn't know what or how to reply. Bewildered, he was looking at her girlfriend like he didn't understand anything.

As Laurie grabbed her keys, Brandon continued to not know what to do or say. It was the first time he saw someone acting like that. Laurie was certain she needed to leave this place and nothing would have stopped her. She left the apartment and looked towards the building. In the apartment below, all the lights were on. It was strange because it was about midnight! Stepping between two realities, a frightened Laurie left the building and silently thanked her neighbor for protecting the door and fighting against the forces of evil...

Rushing to her uncle's house, she was scared while looking at the dark sky. Laurie imagined the presence of an invisible dome around her and her car. It made her feel more safe until she arrived at her Aunt Angela's home.

~ 10 ~

In the Spiritual Dimension

When Laurie finally arrived at her destination, all the lights were off. She entered through the downstairs of the house and she was surprised to see her cousin sitting on the couch in the dark, breastfeeding her baby.

"Excuse me, Val, I didn't mean to scare you."

Éric, Valerie's husband, came out of the room to see what was going on as Peter walked halfway down the stairs. He asked his goddaughter with a comforting voice what she was doing there. With dry tears on her cheeks, Laurie joined him upstairs. Peter wasn't too surprised to see her in this state of mind after the day she had. He asked warmly,

"What's going on, Laurie?"

"I was afraid at home. You may find it strange... but I had the impression that something evil was trying to chase me and bring me with him." Laurie stated freely, unafraid of his judgment since they have always been so close.

Uncle Peter asked again if she had taken drugs.

"No, I swear."

Changing the subject, Laurie continued seriously, "When I left the apartment, the neighbor's lights were all on! They know about the door between the two worlds, because they are protecting it. But I don't know for how long they will hold. They seemed so tired lately."

Laurie gave her uncle a moment so he could realize the magnitude of the situation.

"That's why I don't want to sleep at home. I don't know how long evil will chase me. I don't know what we can do. Who can help us?"

Peter had nothing to add, so he stood up. "It's getting late. We should talk about it in the morning."

Because his daughter Valérie and Éric were sleeping in the guest room, Peter offered Laurie to sleep in the living room on a reclining chair. He apologized for not doing more.

Confused, Laurie wondered, *What more could he do?*

Peter put a cozy, cotton blanket on his goddaughter, who then looked at him straight in the eyes to show him that she was feeling better already. She thanked him, adding that this place is going to be perfect. Peter leaned towards her and gave her a little love tap on her shoulder.

"Okay, try to sleep now. We're right next door if you need us. Tomorrow is going to be a better day."

Feeling overwhelmed by emotion, Laurie added nothing.

From her room, aware of the situation, Angela prayed upon her mother and her sister to protect Laurie.

Laurie didn't want to close her eyes because it felt strange to sleep somewhere else. She looked around at the room thinking about Brandon. *He's probably furious with me.* She looked through the patio door next to her and instantly became fascinated by the view. It was as if the images had been exaggerated or altered by fantastic special effects. Laurie's eyes immediately widened because the vista was breathtaking. The reflection of the full moon sparkled on the little pond. The light of the moon enlightened the dark, and she could see the church and the cemetery on the mountain. Higher to the top, the red light of the cross was clearly glowing in the night. The poet's side in her described it as a beacon in the dark, and it gave her a sense of comfort. She realized how lucky people from Aliville were to have such a sacred symbol.

Above, the moon lit up the sky, the stars were extraordinarily bright. Laurie contemplated the sky until it seemed that the profile of the lookout points further on the mountain appeared in her field of vision to be more gigantic than usual. She enjoyed the view without questioning why this fantastic visual effect appeared to her. Recalling the views of many towns from this place, she thought it was just wonderful, and moved her gaze to find something else to contemplate.

Her mind wandered to the cemetery at the church where the urn containing the ashes of her mother, the bones of her grandmother Marie-

Ange, her grandfather William, and Joseph (her mother's stillborn little brother)

Mystically, the word "Joseph" reverberated in Laurie's mind. She wanted to understand why it resonated so much. Somehow, the energy around sounded to suggest "Jesus." Confused, she questioned, *baby Joseph or baby Jesus?* Only a second passed, then the name Marie-Ange resonated like Mary, *Marie-Ange or Mother Mary?* Suddenly, a vision of the back of a woman, expressing kindness and comfort appeared. All Laurie could see was a long blue veil covering the hair of a woman that fell on either side of her arms as well as her upper body. The lady was moving like she was rocking a baby. Laurie was so confused because it looked more like Mother Mary who had saved her when she was seventeen than her actual grandmother, which she was thinking about while looking at the cemetery.

Laurie finally began to believe the generations before her were perhaps the Holy Family! *Grandmother, is you Mother Mary?* Reflecting on the fact that she had been able to see her grandmother a few times after her death, so big and so clearly in the sky. As well as her secret miracle when Mother Mary had appeared once to protect her from evil entities, Laurie imagined it was possible. She asked again, *Is that right? Am I right Grandma? Is you Mother Mary?* Like a vision, Marie-Ange immediately appeared above her granddaughter, with her usual white curly hair, but this time she looked at her differently, and seemed to say, *Yes, in a way I am both!*

Pleasantly stunned by the answer to her question, Laurie felt an immense joy of life. And believing she had discovered her grandparents' identities, Laurie's heart seemed to beat a thousand times per second while no longer did she contemplate any barriers between the physical world and the spiritual world. Her brain and logic had fallen into a pause mode; Laurie was free and saw the world with the eye of her soul.

Laurie was still looking out the window at the immensity of the sky when a huge ball of white light appeared and moved toward the lookout point. The light settled down on the platform; creating an enormous vibration before her gaze finally followed the dazzling light. Laurie thought that everyone around the area had to have been awakened because it had become so illuminating outside and because of the vibration, like an earthquake, had been so intense. Laurie imagined people getting up from bed going out to the street to take a closer look at it. She wanted to get up and go, but her instinct told her to stay and to watch carefully what was about to be shown.

Amazingly, Laurie thought because she had discovered the mystery of her grandmother, she was allowed to see more. A vague image that lasted for a while appeared behind that piercing light. When the image became clearer, Laurie was stunned to see a statue, which looked like the same one that dominates the city of Rio de Janeiro; the one representing Christ the Redeemer with his arms held open horizontally like a cross, expressing power and freedom.

Laurie felt something powerful was happening, but wondered, *How could this be real?* She questioned herself, *It cannot be my imagination, I could never have imagined such a phenomenon!* She wondered how the other people were reacting to this apparition. Her instinct seemed to suggest nobody had seen it because the statue appeared in the other world, another dimension, and only Laurie could see it since she had discovered the secret. With all these unbelievable questions without answers, Laurie happily decided to wait until the morning to see the reaction of people. *Did they see it, too?*

As if to get back Laurie's attention, the dazzling light surrounding the statue transformed and seemed to represent her mother's energy. Smaller, in front of Hetty, an image of a boy's body appeared wearing a crown of thorns on his head. Laurie could hardly believe what she was seeing, and wondered if it was her brother or Jesus. The male body started to wobble in the light in such a way that it began to change into a female image; the crown of thorns had disappeared along with the male image. While Laurie was watching the phenomenon carefully, it was her own face and body that she was starting to see. Laurie wasn't questioning anymore, and only admired the phenomenon that was shown. It was the most magnific show she had ever seen. The sky was covered with magic; there were millions of stars, and the Northern Lights were dancing. The energies of the statue, the masculine and the feminine were transformed into rays of light, showing a fusion of colors. Spellbound by this phenomenon, her mind was suggesting she had witnessed what was the Trinity.

Laurie's spirit was satisfied, but her brain was destabilized. She wanted to rest, but she couldn't. Somehow, the idea of the four rays of light that had appeared from the Heaven to the Earth during her mother's burial, became stronger and suggested; that it was a code sent to those two paralleled worlds, to prophesy that in four years from that day, the mystery of the Holy family will be revealed.

Laurie was ecstatic about this idea. She was certain she wasn't hallucinating because the visions throughout her life and the four rays had been real and seen by her family. Happy, she wondered, *Why am I seeing those incredible phenomena?*

But without notice, Laurie's mind propelled itself like a rocket into the Universe... Perhaps because she accepted one reality of another dimension, she was allowed to see another one...

In a Superior Dimension; The Galaxy

Laurie's soul had been propelled high up in the dark space of the galaxy. Incredibly, she was thousands of miles away from earth, outside her body. She felt weightless and wasn't seeing anything around her, not even her physical body. She was floating in the air, in a blue dark space. Her consciousness had somehow managed to keep up with this experience and wondered, *What am I doing here in space?* While looking directly at the stars that were appearing, she realized she didn't need to breathe.

It felt like only a second had passed. Laurie's soul was back in her body, and she was back looking at the patio door. She felt like she could vomit because, even though it was an out of body experience, her body felt like it was real. It was too much to handle; the experience of being propelled deep into the atmosphere, followed by being weightless up there for a moment, and then falling in a flash from so high up. It was like the feeling of being on a huge roller coaster; you fall back but your heart stayed up at the top and it takes your breath away.

In a fit of panic, Laurie wanted and needed to know, *What just happened?* She pressed her head on the chair and breathed deeply.

Her soul moved again at the speed of light. In a split second, Laurie was in nothingness again. Floating in the galaxy, she was aware that she went through countless miles and years; billions of kilometers from earth. She realized that during this passage, she had been seen by several archaic people. In a flash, she had distinctive images of an Indian chief, a Neanderthal man, an alien and finally a small man; like a Chinese man. She felt them strongly spiritually. During her brief contact with them, she had seen the surprise on their faces. She had surprised them. They all, and each of them in turn, followed her with their gaze during her fleeting visit. In hindsight, Laurie saw herself looking at them with an interrogative look. *What's going on? What am I doing here?* Then, she had the impression that they sent her a message: "Don't worry, it's rare, but this phenomenon is harmless!"

Alone in weightlessness, Laurie felt so light. She realized again that she didn't need to breathe. Everything was black around her. She had no idea where she was in the Universe. She didn't even know where to go or what to do. Worried she could be going crazy, she asked for help. Then she felt pressure on her right temple, so she paid attention to the phenomenon... A small beige-brown dog with a flattened nose appeared in her thought. He was running towards her. Laurie intended to ignore it, but he then presented himself as bigger and more aggressive as he kept running towards her. As a physical reflex, she pushed him strongly with the palm of her right hand as if it were approaching for real. Laurie felt her heart beating hard due to fear, so she kept her arm in this defensive position for a moment.

She heard a noise similar to a click, giving the impression an old watch had just started the time. From this phenomenon, Laurie understood her physical action with the dog had started a kind of mechanical action. The phenomenon moved around her stomach. As Laurie was trying to understand this sensation, she felt like a giant, like she was looking at the galaxy from above the Universe. When she moved her gaze down towards her sudden transparent stomach, instead, she was seeing the galaxy! She saw particles come together and align so that a circular ring was formed around her, moving in a counterclockwise direction. While trying to understand more, she saw the dog reaching the ring, and calmly, he took a sitting position as if he would stay there forever. Laurie thought she was about to witness how the constellations had been positioned in space as part of creation. As a result of this beauty, she felt like she understood why the Chinese had incorporated the twelve Chinese signs into their culture.

Dizzy and before fainting, she saw again the dragon standing behind her back like she had seen a few years ago.

When Laurie woke up from her out of body experience a moment later, everything was blurry and completely beige. The surreal place was like she was weightless. As she was walking forward, there were four silhouettes on her right-side, all-in line and shoulder to shoulder. The closer Laurie got to them, the more she was able to distinguish them. They were the same spiritual masters that she had just briefly seen earlier when she felt she had been pushed into space.

Mentally, Laurie straightened her body to have an upright posture. She was ready to greet them with the utmost respect. With his mind, the small Chinese man told her to approach him. So, she did but in a slow motion to make sure she could appreciate the moment, or rather, to make sure that she was in control of her mind. The man was shorter than her but bigger. He was wearing square black glasses and a black suit. He was holding in his hands a golden crown, decorated with about an inch sized red stone, and two other smaller blue stones on each side. Laurie wondered how old it was. At first glance, it seemed dull and modest. Then, she began to perceive the crown differently; it had become bright and lustrous, and incredibly, the stones were seemingly coming to life.

In a very kind way, the little man made a solemn nod of the head and motioned for her to imitate him and lean towards him to accept the gift. *What?* The three other beings also bowed their heads to encourage her to do the same. What a wonderful and incredible surprise Laurie felt when she realized that they were there to honor her with a crown. *Perhaps it's because I traveled through time and through the Universe?* She was emotionally moved as she bowed to receive the crown.

Laurie was back in her body, sitting on the chair, wondering why she experienced such an event. Not knowing what ended the marvelous spiritual meeting, she tried to understand if she had an inner need to be recognized. Could she have fabricated the scenario? She didn't think so, and instead, the book story of Richard Bach, *Jonathan Levingston Seagull* came to her, reminding her what the master had said to the seagull: "Your mind allowed you to see what you can see." Grateful, Laurie took this as her answer to why she had lived this incredible supernatural marvelous moment.

She accepted the fact she had actually seen those spiritual masters and had travelled into space and into eras. But it was too much. She wanted to sleep, but her mind wouldn't allow it. Without any control over her thoughts, she was revisiting moments of her childhood.

She was playing with her brother in the basement of their house. Both sitting on the grey carpet, him playing war with his G.I. Joe toys, and her playing spraying love with her Barbies. Laurie remembered the feeling of pride to be hanging out with her big brother.

Slowly, she was transported upstairs, and she revisited the day she was about five-years-old and had daydreams about her Grandfather William. Her mom, Hetty, was crying, and Laurie had asked her why she was so sad. Her mom responded by hugging her daughter tightly that she was missing her father very much. Laurie had looked up at her mom, and confessed she was speaking to him sometimes before falling asleep.

"Who are you talking to before you fall asleep?" Hetty had questioned, holding back tears so as to not frighten her little girl.

"To Grandpa."

In a thoughtful way, Hetty sat her daughter on the counter near the sink to be face to face with her.

"How do you know who he is? You weren't even a year old when he passed!"

Laurie had opened the cupboard door behind her, pointed at the picture of a man and said,

"I talk to him."

Feeling she was being reprimanded, sobs had begun to change the tone of her voice,

"And you told me he is your father and my grandfather."

Hetty immediately hugged her daughter and consoled her while trying to hide her tears.

"For how long have you been talking to him?"

Laurie had shrugged her shoulders since she didn't know what to say. Time didn't really matter at this age.

"I don't understand! He listens to me when I'm sad, and he tells me stories. He is my friend!" She had finally explained impatiently.

Later that evening, from her room, Laurie had heard her parents discuss a perceived problem, and Laurie's greatest sadness was that her grandfather was telling her that it was time for him to go away now. She had taken those words as a farewell. Days later, her dad Stephane had tried to talk to her about the grandfather, but she had told him with frustration that her grandfather was gone.

Laurie remembered she had never talked about those daydreams since. And while sitting on her aunt's chair, Laurie realized she had totally forgotten about that episode, and she was so surprised to remember that moment now. *Why now?* She reflected.

Without a break, like the connection from one episode to another was being explained, Laurie was transported to the school she attended in second grade. She was revisiting the day she had met with a young girl who seemed to be a good and cheerful person, and she remembered how much she wanted to be friends with her. A few days later, this girl was sitting on a tree trunk waiting for buses to arrive. Laurie was looking at her, wondering how to approach her. In fact, Laurie was about to give up and leave but from that moment on, with a greater view, she saw herself being pushed by an invisible phenomenon; a delicate but firm thrust that had led her to her future best friend. While remembering that moment, she understood why it had been so easy.

At the thought, Laurie leapt in the chair; *It's like the same push I received at the airport in Hawaii! And then with Brandon, at the funeral home. Wow!* She exclaimed, waiting for the vision to continue.

Timidly she had stepped closer and had asked Arianne if she wanted to play with her and her friends, but Arianne was waiting for her sister. With a timid and happy warm smile, Arianne had asked Laurie if she wanted to wait with her and had made a place for her to sit on the tree trunk. Ever since that day, they were best friends.

Believing it was magnificent, Laurie thanked her grandfather, *You chose the best friend for me!* Feeling serene about it, she felt the intensity of her grandfather entering inside her space. She couldn't see him but felt as if he winked tenderly at her while expressing, *You had already chosen her, you just needed a little push!*

Laurie burst as reunification with her grandfather was taking place. *I truly had these conversations with you!* She felt so privileged, and she understood that from those back-to-back visions that were deliberately shown to her, he had guided her to connect with people from her world instead of contemplating a different one.

William brought his granddaughter with him into a deeper level of subconscious. He wanted her to know what was happening during all of his visits. Yes, he had listened to Laurie telling him how she wanted peace and love over war; how troubled she felt at hearing arguing; how much she wanted her grandmother to not be paralyzed. *Yes, that's right, that's what I was sharing with you.*

With teary eyes of fatigue and joy, comfortably sitting and remembering these discussions, Laurie wanted to remember what he told her in return, in order to confirm that it was not only one way... and that it wasn't her imagination.

As if a passage had opened, Laurie had her answers; behind each of the stories he had told her, he had prepared her for this moment that would soon arrive... *September 2012, the supposed end of the world according to many!* He had taught Laurie lessons with the games Risk and Chess to integrate in her the principle of strategy. He had told her about the stars and the universe. Laurie felt he had also taught her wisdom.

On this, the energy left. Alone with her thoughts, she remembered her cousins and her brother playing in the living room of her grandmother's house. The boys were playing strategy and war games, and they didn't want Laurie to play with them because she was too young. *That's probably why my grandfather was playing with me in my daydream?* Laurie questioned but had no answer. She wondered if her cousins had daydreams about Grandfather William, too. *If so, do they remember it?*

~ 12 ~

It's Too Much!

It was 5 a.m. and Aunt Angela stood next to Laurie and noticed her tears. She had a vague idea of why Laurie was sleeping on the living room chair, but curious she asked,

"What's going on Laurie? Have you been crying?"

Surprised she hadn't heard her coming, Laurie wiped her face.

"I was thinking of Grandfather William."

Instead of asking why she was thinking of William, in a quiet voice Angela said,

"It's five o'clock in the morning. I'm not going back to sleep. Do you want to rest in the bed next to your godfather?"

"Yes, thank you. I really need to sleep!" Laurie said gratefully while standing up a little dizzy.

Laurie finally laid down horizontally on her belly, which was her favorite sleeping position. She felt at peace, like her body and mind were transported to heaven. The mattress was comfortable, and she noticed Uncle Peter began to snore. She looked at him, observing his body shape in the near darkness. Laurie's heart began to beat faster when she saw two dragons above them. They bickered, trampling over the bed to find sufficient space for them both. Laurie held her breath—hoping they wouldn't see her. After a few seconds, somehow Laurie found the strength to look at one of them and observe his behavior.

The beast on top of Uncle Peter was brown with a shade of blue and his muzzle was somewhat round. Laurie was frightened but at the same time, by looking at him, she didn't sense any evil lurking within him. It seemed as if he wanted to play. He started to flap his wings and then, blue and green radiant colors, supernatural and intense started to blend with the other colors. Bewitched by this emanating beauty and power, Laurie lowered her gaze, not because the light was too bright but because she doubted she was allowed to look at this divine creature.

After a few seconds, she felt as if he was allowing her to observe him. Laurie took advantage of the opportunity and watched him in awe. She felt somewhat privileged but at the same time, she wondered what his shell was made of, since it seemed to be soft, even with the visible crevices. She wanted to touch him but resisted her inner urge. Then a thought came to her; *What if, when he feels no fear, he portrays these vibrant and amazing colors, but when he protects himself, the fabrics would magically change like a chameleon—transforming into something solid and unwavering, dull, and colorless, to frighten his opponents—or maybe he has the ability of becoming invisible?* She believed her thoughts to be true. She felt fortunate that this creature shared his tenderness and vulnerable side with her. She was about to cry out in joy but when she noticed the shape of his belly, almost pear-shaped, she burst out in laughter. He had a potbelly like Uncle Peter. With her beliefs of Chinese signs, she was astonished to think he shared the same shape of Peter. *And the imminent blue of his color was related to Peter's water bottling business.*

She never questioned herself as to why she was seeing dragons. No, she was amazed at how her uncle's physical appearance was familiar to this creature above him. She then wondered what the creature on top of her looked like. Strangely, even lying on her stomach, she was able to see him. Immediately it began to spread his massive wings, then stretch his neck until he touched the ceiling with the tip of his nose. With his long-necked body shape, she realized he could have stretched even more if it hadn't been for the limited ceiling space! Also, he could have released a stream of flames to create more space if he chose to do so. Instead, his entire body; his long tail and huge powerful wings changed colors beautifully into a bright red, mixed with light orange. The brilliant colors resembled a sharp fire. This vision was astonishing to Laurie! She had no words to describe this beauty.

As she watched those two dragons with admiration, her mind propelled back in time to the prehistoric era of the mighty dinosaurs. She didn't want to be there, and she fought with her consciousness. She demanded to sleep rather than to be there! *After all, the dinosaur era was more of my brother's interest!* During the battle with her mind, a little girl appeared. She popped into her mind to say she was curious and wanted to know more about the days of the dinosaurs. Laurie ignored her and looked at the clock—it was 5:30 a.m.

The two dragons were still in the room. The one lingering over Peter had decided to rest. He had laid his belly and small paws on the mattress and finally, in a rather comical motion, dropped the underside of his jaw on the pillow. His left paw was on top of Peter's left hand. Laurie observed both bodies; *One inside the other? Or one on top of the other?* Her vision was once again three dimensional. She understood this phenomenon to be wonderful and real at the same time. They were so similar that she had no difficulty in considering them as one; to be the same soul, who lives in different bodies throughout time, and could meet at the same time in a parallel world.

While she scrutinized her own other presence, she was surprised he had remained seated since the impression was that he could flee at any moment, and release whatever destruction he wanted. He seemed so powerful and upset seconds ago and now he was seated, appearing years away in his thoughts. Because she believed in the theory of space-time relativity, she had an idea that two of her etheric bodies had met again. Laurie felt like he was waiting for her. *But why?*

She was passionately looking at the dragon over her but unfortunately, he seemed as if he was feeling imprisoned in this room. She wondered if in his other life he was feeling trapped, too. Laurie wanted both bodies to feel at peace, so she took several deep breaths and tried, through her thoughts, to calm her other presence. It was difficult, as he seemed to be experiencing frustration that she didn't recognize. Laurie focused on her breathing again and her inner thought-power traveled to her stomach.

In one massive leap, Laurie got up. Tears of fatigue rose within her and both corners of her eyes were wet. She could barely see where she was moving. She felt like she couldn't take it anymore—She was going to explode! Laurie hurried out of the room as she passed next to Angela who was sitting quietly on the reclining chair. As she walked to the kitchen exit door, Laurie's voice trembled,

"Excuse me Angela. I really have to go outside before I go crazy!"

Once outside, Laurie felt instant relief. Space and fresh air. The sun was rising. Laurie went to the same place, near the pond, stood where she found the perfect view of the mountain with all its symbols that could comfort her. She looked up to the sky searching for the dragon, but he had left freely.

Similar to her experience the noon before, Laurie's body began to tremble, and a powerful force burst under the ground and began to pass through her. Laurie's entire body was shaking as she followed this new rhythm. The energy vibrated under the words of an old foreign language. The sounds that came from her body were explosive, insistent, and broken. It was like stretching an emotional vowel one at a time. Differently than the day before, she was looking straight ahead at the mountain, instead of at the sky. The screams were not as loud; however, the feelings were much more intense, as if some energy was stored within her. Laurie felt as if souls were under the ground. Souls who wanted to pass through her opening to be released from the darkness. She could feel the earth vibrating under her feet, thinking these souls longed to tell her something like—*let us help you!* The sound she was making was still resounding. Everything was intensely vibrating inside her!

The more she allowed these vibrations to be expressed, the more she felt an entire population was free and at peace. They were thanking her, providing her strength and courage to accomplish what she was supposed to do next. Even Mustang, Peter's Golden Retriever, had become fond of Laurie, seeming to understand these odd events. Without any barking, curious, Mustang sat next to her, ears straight in the air as if it seemed to be waiting for something, or maybe he was protecting her. Laurie's hands vibrated and responded to this power belonging to a different dimension, which seemed to come from the interior earth. *Or could it be the magic of an ancient ritual evoked hundreds of years ago? Why not?* Laurie was thinking while allowing her body to be possessed. *The Aboriginals had a better connection with the earth than todays' people. They believed in breaches in time!* Laurie was thinking while living this incredible moment.

Exhausted, Laurie had finished screaming and vibrating. She thought she had to redistribute these energetic forces stored in her body on a pure land. She remembered, *Here is pure land!* Despite her ninety-six hours without sleeping, Laurie found the strength and courage to give back to the earth. She hastened, began to walk around her aunt's property, physically pretending to give seeds of energy back to earth. To make sure to cover the entire perimeter of this land, she even passed behind a shed instead of the easy access in front. Followed by Mustang, she felt like she had done this ritual in another life.

Once the first round of the property was done, the sun was more visible in the sky. It wasn't clear to Laurie if she needed to do a second tour but to feel safe, she continued. Mustang didn't accompany her this time which made her doubt her decision. While continuing to walk and give back to the earth, Laurie became anxious, realizing she had probably woken up her host family with her long one minute or so of screaming. She looked at the sky to ask for help, but she saw the big bird again—this bird of doom belonging to that of evil! The same evil that had made so much noise last night before opening the door between the two worlds. Laurie was frightened at the thought he had found her and might try to catch her. She began to walk faster and desperately prayed that God would help her accomplish her important mission.

In the meantime, Angela was talking to Brandon over the phone, alarming him about Laurie's incomprehensive behavior and her screaming again. In disbelief, Valérie was sadly looking at her cousin walking on the land, and gesturing like she was spraying seeds all around the property. Éric was taking care of the babies, putting them back to bed, and Peter had left for a quick office job.

When Laurie finally arrived near the front of the entrance, she collapsed with fatigue. She fell on the lawn, knees first, hands and then head. She released a deep sigh of relief. *I've done the job; I can rest now!* Crouching on the ground as she caught her breath, the image of the galaxy along with the position of the stars, and the origin of the Chinese signs she had missed last night, came back to her mind! Laurie had just stepped into another world. She remembered vaguely witnessing the Big Bang and the origin of the Chinese sign. Mustang was already next to Laurie. She wondered which sign would come next after the dog.

A second later, Laurie was very happy to see her cousin coming out of the house, confirming she was the next one. Valérie bent and covered her trembling cousin with a blanket and asked her if she was okay. With a faint smile, Laurie replied that she was fine while perceiving how amazingly powerful her old-soul-of-a-cousin was. With wet eyes and her compassionate smile, Valérie warmly asked, "Do you want to go inside? It's kind of cold this morning!" With a positive response, Valérie helped her tired cousin to her feet, supporting her as they walked to the house. During this quick walk, Laurie tried hard to remember her young cousin's Chinese sign but had no idea! Laurie was trying to find out what would be the next sign to come...

Before the cousins walked through the door, Laurie heard this familiar engine noise. It was Brandon in his van. She was thrilled to see the tiger sign coming! Once inside, Angela was standing up, waiting in silence. Laurie squinted, *What's her sign?* Still, she had no idea. Laurie was looking for her uncle in the room and didn't see him. *That's right, there can't be two dragons!* Laurie concluded.

Éric joined them to find out about Laurie's health. He was a firefighter by profession who exuded a calm presence and prominent security, which Laurie appreciated. Brandon entered the house without knocking, as if he knew most of them were waiting for him. He requested Laurie to sit on the wooden bench by the kitchen counter.

Angela, in her usual calm tone, said, "Laurie, you are not well."

Brandon was extremely nervous. He was searching for words so as not to be too direct,

"Lo, I called the police! Either you decide for yourself to go to the hospital, or we will force you to go. It's no longer just for your safety, but for the safety of others as well," he explained.

Laurie looked at him with pure love. He was there to help her. He was worried about her. She let him speak, admiring him even more.

"Lo, what you are doing is not rational. You need help!"

"I'm fine. I just need to take a shower and get some sleep and I'll be better," Laurie said while making eye contact with Valérie and Éric.

Their concerned faces were filled with compassion. They didn't know what to say. Laurie became emotive. Tears swelled into her eyes while asking,

"What do you think? Do you think I should go to the hospital?"

Without a word, everyone nodded, providing Laurie with an affirmative answer.

Peter arrived, and Laurie asked for his opinion. His facial expression revealed that he did not understand her behavior, so he said,

"I don't know. I don't know what's happening to you!"

Laurie finally looked at her godmother who kindly said,

"I think you might need it."

Tears streamed down even more as she was attracting everyone's emotions. Laurie looked out the window and saw this bird of doom in the sky. It looked like the evil was getting closer to her and she was no longer safe in this open land. She had to find a place to hide! *The hospital! The hospital would be perfect! Plus, I need some rest, and a time out!* Laurie was realizing it was meant to be as she was guided to this much needed place of rest. But she looked at them again, one by one; Brandon, Angela, Valérie, Éric, and Peter. They were all standing in front of her, with a deep desire to help her.

"Are you sure about that? Do you really think I could be better off in the hospital?"

Brandon seemed to be praying that she would say yes, as if that was the only way he could breathe again. Angela and Valérie, almost with tears in their eyes, nodded yes. Éric seemed to be telling, *Girl, you have no choice!* Peter probably was thinking, *I'm not happy with what's happening to you. I feel sorry for you, but I think you should listen to what they all tell you!*

Uncomfortable on the small round wooden stool, Laurie accepted it.

As she said, "Well, okay. I'm ready!" She sensed they were all relieved, and even more Brandon, realizing no violence or force would be necessary.

Laurie and Brandon left in his white van. Mentally exhausted, Laurie was between two worlds: her present world and within the history of Brandon's novel... Her thoughts were elsewhere and so were his. However, Brandon had taken the trouble to turn off the radio. Laurie had noticed it and began to think he wanted to hide from her the journalists comments on the phenomenon of the day before; the appearance of the statue of the Christ settled on the viewpoint of the Mount Mirabaska! Neutral, Laurie thought, *We're going to get in front of it anyway so, I'll be able to see for myself!*

It was a brief ride between her uncle's house and the hospital that was located down below on the mountain. On the way, Laurie saw no statue, crowds, or media. She glanced back at the road in front of her.

Too exhausted, she couldn't feel yet the powerful energy of her grandmother that was waiting for her at the hospital...

~ 13 ~

Hospitalization

Coincidently or not, it had passed exactly four years the day before Laurie's mom had passed away, and exactly two years when Laurie and Brandon had met for the first time. It was at her cousin Steve's funeral service. Laurie had moved to stand alone and stepped back away from the coffin. In peace, she listened to the distinct voices of her dad, his sibling, and her cousins who shared greetings and grief with friends and family who had come to offer their sincere condolences. As she sensed the air in the funeral home felt warm, her thoughts had turned to memories of her mother. With tears in her eyes, she was remembering the supernatural moment when she saw her mother's soul passing into the other world. Following the heart of these thoughts, she looked at her cousin's inanimate body while trying to get an image of the people who he had now reached on the other side. But no visions had appeared to her this time. She fluttered her eyelids, and her tears dried as she was removed from her ideas.

A young man had entered the room and stood before the deceased with his head bowed and his hands reverently held together in front of him, showing his sadness and respect. This guy was crying a few steps away from Laurie who noticed his well combed hair, and the stylish way he was dressed, but most part, he seemed so sad. He was there to mourn the departure of his friend. As a sign of respect, Laurie also looked down and held her hands together. Standing straight and with her feet firmly grounded, Laurie continued to pray silently to God and to Mother Mary to keep the soul of her cousin in their divine light, to love him, to comfort him and to guide him. Just at that exact moment, unexpectedly and despite her anchored position, in her back, Laurie received a firm invisible thrust that drove her within two steps of this kindly gentleman. Too late to back away—he had already seen her right next to him! And it was how their journey had begun.

***

Tuesday, May 15, 2012

"I called earlier, and I already explained the situation to you." Brandon was telling the secretary at the emergency registration desk, while Laurie was experiencing hot and cold flashes, with her ideas somewhere else.

"Of course, I remember you. Do you have Miss Laurie Lora's identity cards?"

Uncertain, Brandon asked his girlfriend if she had brought her purse, and he asked for her papers. Thinking he was asking her for the papers she had grabbed in a hurry, just before leaving her apartment the day before, Laurie immediately gave him the phone numbers of three mystical friends she thought could be helpful in case she disappeared from this world.

"What is that?" Brandon asked. Realizing the nonsense of the situation, and unsure how to react, Brandon smirked and added, "I only want your health insurance card."

As Laurie was coming back to this reality, also realizing the stupidity of the situation, embarrassed, she gave him what he needed.

Waiting for a doctor in Room B, Laurie tried to explain what had happened in the morning, but Brandon didn't seem interested at all. She changed the subject, but still he wasn't attentive until a nurse arrived and asked them to follow her. They walked into another room for an evaluation, and Laurie was asked to lie down on the bed until she'd meet with the doctor.

Moments later, the door opened, and Laurie was dazzled by the sight before her. A ray of light that seemed to come from the heavens was connecting directly to the Doctor who was slowly approaching and introducing herself. In a flash, Laurie understood that higher beings were also coming to examine her physical and emotional state after being used as a lightning rod to liberate the earth, or whatever the reasons were. In this train of thought, telepathically, Laurie began to share with her doctor that she felt good and remembered her out-of-body travels as well.

But when Doctor Paris asked her first question, Laurie was unsettled. *Is it possible that an "angel doctor" really exists? Doctor Paris seems so intelligent and human!* Physically, she looked a lot like her best friend, Arianne, and moreover, they had the same last name. *It's a sign!* Laurie thought, and readily accepted this idea and began to answer the questions aloud. Brandon, who was sitting in a chair further away, had approached to validate each of Laurie's answers.

Once the doctor left, Laurie could finally relax and try to rest. Thinking that she had given her best, she hoped to soon receive the diagnosis of the spiritual world, and understand why these phenomena had happened to her.

As the patient began to close her eyes, another doctor that specialized in mental health entered the room. Doctor Dion wasn't smiling as she seemed rather interested in knowing more about the reasons for Laurie's visit than making a good impression. Brandon began by briefly telling the doctor what his girlfriend had recently done and spoke; then sadly said, "I don't know what is happening to her. I've known her for two years and I can tell you she's not in her normal state of mind!"

Laurie finally stood up and joined the conversation. Strangely, Doctor Dion had put her left hand as if to block Laurie from advancing towards her, but in fact, she was using her hand as a shield to block the strong energy coming from her patient. Laurie felt strong, powerful, filled with energy, and began to speak from her perspective; the authentic truths as to what she had seen and experienced lately.

Doctor Dion was listening carefully to the hasty and unrealistic speeches her patient was telling. After about half an hour of listening without interruption, she suggested to Miss Lora that it would be in her best interest to spend some time at the hospital in order to know more about what is happening. The three of them came to an agreement and Brandon was tasked the responsibility to deliver his girlfriend to her assigned room, but never mentioned floor six—the floor which housed the mental health cases.

As they entered the elevator, Laurie had somehow forgotten where they were going and why. Strangely, she had in mind they were going to visit her grandmother on floor five. Being sometime between two realities, having no barrier of the mind, Laurie was talking freely to Brandon about the difference between the two doctors they met with in the morning; Doctor Paris was a "angel doctor" who came directly from Heaven, and Doctor Dion was a human from this world. Brandon was simply smiling, and nodding as if he understood exactly what she was saying. But in fact, Brandon was relieved from the burden he was carrying lately. Laurie's strange behaviors were confirmed to be taken seriously and she was now at the right place to receive the help she so needed.

When the elevator doors opened on floor sixth, something was wrong... Laurie had never been on this floor. Carefully she followed Brandon. Two other automatic doors opened and there was a nurse waiting for them on the other side. Shaking, Laurie stopped as only now she realized where she was headed. As if she had just completely returned into the physical world and had left behind all her spiritual thoughts. She couldn't hold it, and immediately burst out as she realized she was wrongly diagnosed with mental health problem.

She looked at Brandon who was trying to hold his tears, feeling so sorry for what was happening to his girlfriend. Laurie rushed towards him and tried to muffle the sound of her screams in between his chest. Even with this calming gesture, her cries echoed throughout the entire hospital floor. She realized the commotion she was making but couldn't stop. Feeling overwhelmed, Laurie felt like it was more than her own grief. She felt like all the emotions and memories of other people who had passed this specific threshold point before were reliving in her again. Laurie couldn't keep any of those variety of emotions inside her because it was too massive to endure! Feeling overwhelmed, like her spiritual friend Lisa had advised her once, Laurie looked at the emotions without judging them, let them pass through her, and then she let them go freely by bursting out loud. Physically supported by Brandon, she had no restraint, and let each of the emotions be expressed. This moment was emotionally intense and loud and was frightening numerous people on the floor, including Brandon who was consoling her by hugging her tightly, trying also to reduce the sound of her screams.

Laurie cried for a long time before this sadness was totally liberated. As the last sobs passed, Laurie looked at the nurse who was waiting for her, confirming that she was finally ready to move on.

The nurse had allowed this future patient to pour out all of her sadness before getting closer and introducing herself.

"Hello Laurie. I'm Nurse Caroline. Are you ready to follow me?"

Laurie nodded, wiped away her tears, said a quick goodbye to Brandon, and then followed the nurse.

As they walked through the two large automated blue doors, Laurie saw the corridor dazzle with a white light. She suddenly felt surrounded and enveloped as the light gave her a sense of grandeur and depth, as if the roof and the walls had disappeared. This phenomenon did not surprise her. She felt good in this moment of freedom and felt something was attracting her at the end of the corridor, but the nurse directed her to the first room on the left.

Brandon had watched his girlfriend until she was out of sight. Still at the same position, alone with a discrete tear, Brandon felt overwhelmed with grief seeing Laurie smiling like nothing had happened. He didn't know how to let the pain go, and like many, he just kept everything inside.

As Laurie entered the first hospital room to the left, she instantly lost this presence of vastness and she felt somewhat destabilized, since the ceiling and walls were again around her, solid and designed to limit spaces. Laurie was assigned to the second and last bed in the back of the room, near the huge window. Nurse Caroline asked her to put on the two robes that were placed on the bed and then she compassionately explained how she should be wearing them to hide her back and front. She then suggested with a comforting voice to lie down and try to rest while waiting to see her doctor. As Caroline was closing the curtain, Laurie felt a strong supernatural energy inside the room and wondered if the nurse felt it, too. If so, she found her crafty at keeping her cool.

Once changed, Laurie found a comfortable position on the little mattress. Her head was pushed tightly on the pillow. She looked towards the window to her right and searched in the blue sky for the malefic bird. She was safe because nothing seemed unusual. She folded the wool blanket and pulled it up to her neck, looked up at the ceiling, realizing it was her first time on a hospital bed. She felt euphoric and peaceful at the same time, despite all these continuous unfamiliar noises.

Her eyes were wide open when Doctor Dion arrived.

"Hello Miss Lora. How are you?"

Laurie sat down and Doctor Dion gave her a visual examination. She then calmly told her patient, "Miss Lora, since we don't know exactly what's happening to you yet, I suggest you take this pill that will help you relax and get some sleep."

Laurie didn't like pills. From a young age, she considered most of the pills as a 'band aid' rather than a cure. She took some time before she held out her hand to Doctor Dion to receive the tablet. She was incredulous about the effect and the consequences that medication could have on her. Silently, she encouraged herself saying it was okay for this time. *I think I need it!* She finally managed to swallow the medication after three attempts. The doctor asked her to open her mouth to confirm she had swallowed. She concluded that she would come back to see her in the morning, and that if there is anything she needs, she can ask the nurses to contact her. Doctor Dion was waiting for an answer to make sure her patient understood but Laurie was far in her thoughts, wondering if she had done the right thing by taking the pill. But it was too late; the medication was already flowing through her body.

Seeing the doctor staring at her, Laurie nodded, confirming that she understood. Doctor Dion left; Laurie lied down and fell deeply asleep.

~ 14 ~

Her Grandmother is Mother Mary

When Laurie woke up, she had a terrible splitting headache. Although she put the blame on the medication for this discomfort, she was satisfied she had managed to finally obtain some sleep. It was sunny outside, quiet on the hospital floor and the smell of the food made her realize she was famished. Wondering when the last time she ate, a new nurse arrived with a tray of food, quickly pointing out that normally everyone eats together in the room at the end of the hall. "But today you can eat in your room if you would like." Laurie let her tears flow freely down. Having her meal served in bed, in the hospital, brought her back to reality... *I am hospitalized and I must accept it!*

The nurse left and Laurie began to enjoy the vegetable soup, then savoring the beef cube, mashed potatoes, and peas. Thoughts swirled in her head as she wondered why people said hospital food was bad. She thought the food was delicious. In a strange way, it seemed to her that it was her dear grandmother, Marie-Ange's recipe. Even though she had passed, Laurie had a strong feeling they were using her family recipe. *Maybe during these long hospitalizations, she could have shared her favorite recipes!* Laurie easily believed in that possibility.

Suddenly, her thoughts became blurred. She was reminded vaguely of her conclusion from the evening before; her grandmother was the Holy Virgin Mary. Her logic was struggling to still believe it. But Laurie's spirit instantly flew back in time. She was in her grandmother's room on the fifth floor, revisiting a childhood memory. Despite all the other times she visited her grandmother, it was that moment that she was shown; the moment when she saw for the first time, the kind way Nurse Carmen took care of her grandmother and her paralyzed body.

Carmen! Carmen was her best friend Arianne's mother! In the blink of an eye, Laurie clearly recalled the time when she had found out Carmen was taking care of her grandmother; she was about eight-years-old, visiting Arianne, and had met her friend's mother only a few times. Carmen was dressed in her white nursing uniform, and with her comforting smile she had told Laurie, "Do you know your grandmother, Marie-Ange, is in the hospital?" Shy, Laurie had nodded, wondering how she could know. *Maybe I shared it with Arianne?* "I am taking care of her. I'm her nurse." Carmen had said while noticing the little girl didn't understand, so she added with a laugh, "I was talking with your grandmother about my daughter Arianne's new friend, Laurie. She told me she had a granddaughter also name Laurie, and we found out that we were talking about the same little girl... you." Carmen was also the one who had taught Laurie how to pray to Mother Mary.

Laurie was confused as the vision continued... Carmen was taking care of Marie-Ange and was moving her paralyzed arm. They were smiling at each other, sharing an unconditional love, respect, and kindness. Spectacularly, the image froze on a white screen... it was fuzzy but fantastic. In this moment of greatness, Laurie understood and felt that her grandmother had managed to stop time, and in the pure and divine light, she revealed her identity; Mother Mary was asking Carmen to guide her granddaughter into prayer. After a brief moment of deepness, the image unfroze, and the vision continued. Laurie saw her paralyzed grandmother, complimenting Carmen on her kindness and Catholic values. Stunningly, in a most gentle and warm manner, she was telling her, "With your faith in God, and your great heart, you are truly the person Laurie needs for her journey to Faith."

Mechanically, Laurie's left hand went to her heart to help calm it down. This mind-bending moment stopped. Laurie held her breath, feeling somewhat confused. Not because of her grandmother's authenticity, but this idea that Carmen had known this secret for over twenty-five years and never told her was disturbing. *Does Arianne know it, too? Does she know that my grandmother is the Virgin Mary? Does she know Carmen knows? Does she know that my grandmother asked Carmen to guide me in prayer?*

While Laurie was asking herself all these questions, the memories of praying with Carmen resurfaced in the blink of an eye. Laurie was about eight-years-old and had spent her first weekend at Arianne's house. Arianne had been uncomfortable having to tell her friend that they had to go pray with her family. But Laurie remembered how special that moment had been. She felt delighted about the energy, the warmth of the wood stove in the basement, the way the chairs were placed in circles, and the lights were dimmed. The entire family (the parents and the three sisters) seemed to be at peace, while Laurie did her best to follow and to learn the prayer, "I greet you Mary, full of grace..."

Another significant moment with Carmen appeared. It was a few months later. Arianne was sleeping soundly while Laurie was thinking about her family. Her parents were arguing more often, and she was in a lot of pain. Needing to free herself from that pain, Laurie had responded to the delicate "invisible push," and she joined Carmen in the basement. Trying to hold back her tears, she asked, "Can we pray please?" A bit surprised, Carmen had put her reading away, grabbed her rosary chain, dimmed the light, sat in front of Laurie, and began to pray one whole rosary. Laurie remembered feeling a special sense of pure stillness that day and began to believe that the Virgin Mary had been with them in the room. And then, many other moments with Carmen reappeared, with her solemn air telling Laurie over time, until now, "I will pray for you," was recounted as to conclude and convince Laurie that her vision was real; that indeed, there had been a time when Mother Mary had asked Carmen to guide her in prayer.

Unbelievable! Laurie whispered while being guided to the event that happened to her when she was seventeen-years-old, and black spots like evil entities were flowing around and frightening her. Laurie had prayed like Carmen had taught her, and miraculously, Mother Mary had appeared to Laurie, sweeping away those evil entities and forbidding them to come into Laurie's etheric body again.

Grateful, Laurie took another bite of peas when a powerful energy similar to an earthquake had started to vibrate under the floor. Laurie paid special attention. This energy seemed as if it was coming from the room where her grandmother had spent so much time before on floor five. Then, with all the power created by the vibrations, the energy started to move throughout the corridor and then turned right—just under Laurie's room. Laurie was focused on this immense energy as it traveled. Concerned, she was waiting to find out the result, but it felt like the force had waited for her to be calm and ready before crossing the floor of her room and filling it with pure love.

Stunned by this phenomenon, she realized what had just happened was to prepare a safe place for her. This occurrence was to protect her and make her journey there easier. Laurie shook her head trying to understand more in detail. *Grandmother, did you know back then, when you were hospitalized, that this very moment was about to happen? Did you know I was supposed to come here? Or maybe you just now performed that magic trick?*

There were no answers. Only Laurie had gained more confidence even though the powerful energy in the room was already fading away. Then again, Laurie's mind traveled quickly to a specific time when she was sitting at a church with plenty of people, and in front of her, the priest was saying, "The body of the Christ," while raising his arms to heaven. Immediately after seeing that, Laurie's mind was back in her body and wondered, *Why this vision?* As a response, her consciousness traveled far back in time, in a location that seemed to be in a cave. There were men clothed in long dresses. Some of them were chatting, and the emotions were mixed. Witnessing from above the scene, the vision became clearer as other people were sitting on one side of a long table. Food and wine were abundant.

Back on her hospital bed, Laurie thought she had just witnessed a moment Jesus had shared a meal with his disciples. At this realization, while looking at her own food, she felt like a miracle had just happened on this floor; something as if the food had been improved and would heal everyone who would eat it.

Before she had time to question that idea, Laurie heard a familiar voice in the distance and turned her attention to it. It was Brandon asking the nurse about her. Despite all the noise, people talking and the confusion on the floor, she could hear them clearly, like her auditive perception was fine-tuned. Brandon was asking if his girlfriend would be okay. The nurse's voice was more discreet when she spoke, "Besides telling you that she slept a little this afternoon, I can't tell you more since at the moment, we don't know what she has. And it's her first time here." Resigned, Brandon told the nurse he had brought personal belongings for Laurie. But the nurse kindly asked him to leave it at the counter since she had to check everything and only a few items were permitted in the rooms. "It's for her own safety," she had said.

In the end, Laurie couldn't hear them. She took a bite from her piece of angel cake and was surprised when Brandon entered her room. She was confused as; *Should I be happy to see him or should I be angry with him for bringing me here.* Then she felt his love and heard his calm and reassuring voice asking how she was doing and telling her what he had brought for her. "I know, I heard you talking," she spoke. But Brandon looked at her with a doubtful look, wondering if it was possible to hear from such a distance.

Later, a different nurse arrived to take Laurie's blood pressure, give her a pill, and had made sure the patient swallowed the medication. She reminded Brandon visiting hours were over and he had to leave.

"I'll be back tomorrow," Brandon said with a tear in his eye. It was difficult for him to leave his girlfriend on this floor and even more difficult thinking that she didn't seem concerned about the situation she was in.

The nurse sat on the visitor's chair with a paper and pencil. She asked why she thought she was at the hospital. Laurie sat comfortably on the little bed, ready to chat, as if the nurse was her great friend. Spontaneously and unrestrainedly, Laurie confessed that she was there to rest and to hide from the evil. She shared that her grandmother was Mother Mary and discussed her boyfriend's novel. "Oh yes, he wrote a book?" the nurse asked, visibly surprised to finally hear something that was possibly real.

The sleeping pill began to take effect and the nurse exited the room. Before falling asleep, the patient next to her arrived. They couldn't see each other due to the curtain that separated them. Nevertheless, Laurie told her good night, and she replied in a surprised but sweet voice, "Good night to you, too?"

~ 15 ~

Miracles

When Laurie woke up in the morning, the first thing she did was to look out the window. The sky was blue and cloudless. Strangely, she was happy to wake up at the hospital. As she stretched her entire body, she realized she was no longer feeling as if she was between two worlds. She believed that she had healed and wondered if it was due to having a full night of sleep or maybe it was the sleepy effects of the medication.

Ready to explore the surroundings, but unsure whether she was allowed to leave her room, Laurie leaned against the door frame and took some time to breathe and calm her excitement from within. The corridor seemed inviting. Laurie finally left her room and cautiously walked in the middle of the hallway, peeking into the rooms whose doors were ajar. She walked past the reception desk, which was halfway down the corridor. The nurses turned and seemed surprised to see her there. Laurie smiled at them and went on her merry way. A young man with black hair was coming her way. He had dark brown eyes and a blank look, but as he passed by Laurie, he looked at her with an intense expression as if to intimidate her. He frowned and displayed a sinister smile, revealing his full set of teeth. Laurie wasn't afraid but was rather surprised to feel like she had entered the etheric body of this young man. Curious, she turned to see him continuing his way. He did not turn around and retreated straight to his room. His carefree way made Laurie think he had a great power, and he knew she was watching him.

As she continued walking, Laurie wondered what he had done to her because she had changed. She felt like a sad little girl. Even though she didn't know the guy, she wished he had returned to her, to comfort her and reassure her as a big brother would do. It was an impulse. Laurie yearned to be accepted by him! As she pondered this thought, she looked down. She smiled at the sight of her French pedicure she had done a week prior, just to be prepared for the arrival of hot weather. Quite spontaneously and fortunately, the young woman in her resurfaced. She felt proud and began to walk confidently again. This change in her mood had not worried her.

Laurie finally arrived at the end of the corridor. She would have loved to look by the window, but it was almost impossible because three men were seated on the rocking chairs backed up against the window. And three ladies were sitting on the four straight chairs that were placed on each side of the hallway. Laurie sat on the only empty chair, which was the first one on her left. Behind her, there was another window that had a view of a large room with tables and chairs.

She smiled reservedly at the patients as most of them were friendly to her. *Probably due to my arrival on the floor; they know I'm the one who cried uncontrollably yesterday!* But no one spoke, as disturbing howls had begun to resonate. Intrigued and on the lookout, Laurie looked at the wall in front of her, trying to understand the emotion of the screams expressed by the person in the room. But another different and unfamiliar sound distracted her. The annoying sound was coming from the wheels of a huge portable stainless-steel cabinet pushed by an attendant. He was bringing breakfast and the pleasing smell that reached Laurie's nose helped her calm down. About twelve other hungry patients arrived and gathered around the cabinets, waiting to hear their names to be called. One by one, each patient received their tray and went to sit in the spacious room behind Laurie.

Laurie's name was the last to be called. Standing at the entrance of the grand room with her tray of food in hands, she was looking for the perfect place to sit. There were a few vacant chairs left among three large tables. Happy to meet with her future new friends, Laurie felt good, not feeling any discomfort like when she was a teenager and entered her school cafeteria alone. She glanced over at the third table and confidently headed over, pleased with the view that this location could provide.

As she sat down, she recognized Alexandre, a boy with whom she had gone to high school with. He nodded at her and continued eating. Laurie was content to see at least one familiar face. Next to her, on her right was the boy with dark brown hair whom she met earlier in the corridor. She felt the young man was not happy with her presence, as if he wasn't accustomed to someone sitting beside him! But Laurie didn't mind. She used to often disturb her brother and he never hurt her for invading his space! As she continued to look around, she realized that only a few nurses were talking to their patients and everyone else seemed to be in their own little worlds looking at their plates. Laurie wondered if the people were allowed to chat with each other. Uncertain, she prayed to Mother Mary for a positive change. Amusingly, she had the feeling that her grandmother listened to her prayer and would improve the situation. Laurie peeked around and was happy to see some board games; thinking she might have time to play. Once her breakfast was over, she did like the others did and handed her meal tray to the attendant, thanking her.

"You are welcome. Can you please wear your slippers next time?" The nurse said, seeming a bit irritated.

"But I don't have any!" Laurie said embarrassed.

"Nobody gave you slippers?" Surprised, the nurse asked Laurie to follow her. She gave her a pair of blue paper slippers and Laurie put them on immediately.

When Laurie arrived in her room, two Chinese men in their fifties were inside. One of them was mounted on a stepladder and quickly put back the ceiling tile above her bed. Immediately, Laurie's memory took her to the encounter with the small spiritual being that she had seen when she traveled through space two nights prior; the one who had held the crown. Interestingly, Laurie thought that the Chinese had found her and were installing a camera to get to know her better. *They want to know if I am the one who has traveled through space, and through time!* Amused, Laurie let them do their work, but due to the strange behavior of one of them who turned his back on her as she greeted him, immediately, she believed they were trying to be invisible. But because she could see them, Laurie was amused, and even more amused when they passed beside her to leave the room, acting as if she wasn't there; not looking at her nor excusing themselves for walking so close to her. *Perhaps they had been forbidden to attempt any contact with me?* Laurie gazed at them as they left the room and walked to the edge of the door to see which way they went. She looked both ways but couldn't see them. *It's impossible. Did they just disappear?* Laurie was so amazed thinking the Chinese culture were already working on their power of invisibility or being able to tele transport themselves. Not bothered by the device they had just installed above her bed, she leaned against the door frame, feeling reassured to know they would protect her if she needed help.

Satisfied, she returned to the dining room. It was quiet on the floor, fewer people in the corridor and there was no one inside the big room. Laurie stood gazing at the four large windows behind the second table. There was a beautiful sticker like stained-glass glue on the right window. Oddly, Laurie had the feeling she had to send the energy received from her grandmother into it. While thinking that, somehow, she received a positive confirmation that it was the right time to send a message of love to her family and friends. Even though Laurie had never thought about sending a message to anyone, she followed her instinct and without resistance, she simply let go of her body and her mind in this adventure...

She straightened her body, rooted herself, and took a deep breath ready to let the energy from inside go. Perhaps the medication was interfering because it was unlike the other two times the energy had passed through her. This time she was trying to manifest it—instead of letting it be. With her eyes closed and with all her concentration, she channeled her energy and pushed it toward the stained-glass sticker. While she was aware that energy was finally moving in her heart, she had a vision of a ray of light reaching the stained-glass. It didn't change but on the other side of the window, the stained glass had become a glass prism, and sprayed pure and colorful lights in all directions. Laurie was amazed by the beauty of the lights that manifested outside and how they were gleaming reaching the sky above, trying to cross and connect with the world above. She saw colors that resembled the Northern Lights; transmitting energies of healing, love, and hope. It was so beautiful that Laurie breathed deeply trying to remember this incredible phenomenon forever.

She was aware that someone had opened the door, but something caused this person to retreat. *Maybe that person was afraid of me, or maybe it's because I'm not done, and I need to push more energy?* Uncertain, she continued to send energy to the target. This time, she had the idea that the prism was sending lights to the people of the Earth, and she felt their happiness as they were also witnessing the colorful pure lights reaching from earth to heaven. Incredibly, she felt the people's happiness as it could mean to them; *The Christ is back!*

In Laurie's vision, a crowd of people were coming towards the front of the hospital, attracted by the beauty of lights beaming from the sixth-floor window. Feeling so powerful, Laurie imagined distributing the rest of the energy through the dining room, the corridor, through each room, on each floor, until she felt the hospital was filled with this divine energy. Satisfied, she finished sending the last rays. She walked next to the windows getting prepared to greet these people in the streets and provide them with hope. But once she could see outside, there was no one and no more trace of the spectacular lights. *Perhaps only beings from the other world acknowledged it? Or maybe the people will arrive later?* Then Laurie pondered for a second, if she might have hallucinated, but she put it aside, thinking, *Why would I have hallucinated? And how could I imagine such a phenomenon like that?*

Without a clue, Laurie began to look at the objects placed on the windowsill when two patients entered the room. Slowly, she went back to her room thinking a supernatural force had prevented them from entering the room earlier, so that she could finish her task. Trying to put all this behind her, Laurie got into bed and immediately fell asleep like a baby.

~ 16 ~

Visions

When she woke up, she was confused while seeing a nurse who had arrived. "Hello Miss Lora. I will take your pulse and then you can go have dinner with the others." Laurie lifted her left arm to her while silently wondering, *Did I miss lunch?* It seemed the nurse understood her questioning and simply said, "You slept a good part of the day. That's because you needed it!"

Laurie joined the others for dinner. While eating her first bite, she realized the atmosphere in the dining room had changed from this morning. The nurses were outside in the corridor, and the patients were talking to each other. The mysterious dark-eyed young man beside Laurie immediately looked at her as she turned to him with an interrogative look. She wondered if it was possible... *Could my prayer of this morning have been heard and answered? My prayer asking for a positive change?* Laurie was euphoric thinking it was kind of a miracle. Her smile grew as she looked at her neighbor. Believing he had a superpower, she supposed he knew exactly what was going on but, with the odd look he provided, Laurie felt like he just didn't care! She wondered, *Why does he not care about such a wonderful miracle?* She then thought he might be surrounded by evil souls like she was once, before Mother Mary freed her. *Maybe he deals with it by hiding behind a dark character!* With that in mind, she prayed for him to be freed and protected as she had been.

After dinner, only Alexandre remained in the dining room. He was sitting on one of the two sofas, facing the corridor wall, and was watching the television placed high on a shelf. He seemed embarrassed by Laurie's presence, but she sat down anyway and waited for him to feel comfortable enough before speaking to him.

As she watched the images on TV, Laurie was charmed by the beauty of the Earth and other planets that were shown. Her vision was modified thus seeing in three dimensions a breathtaking view of the Earth; the pale blue colors of the ocean brought out the magnificent Earth from the dark blue of the galaxy. In a split of a second, like she had experienced a few days before at her aunt's house, Laurie's spirit was propelled again into space: to the vastness of the galaxy. This time, she wasn't questioning what was happening. She was simply enjoying the spectacular beauty of the planets in the galactic glory as seen from her location somewhere in the Universe. Laurie felt the effect of weightlessness again, as well as the effect that time did not exist.

It was at that moment Alexandre felt comfortable with her by his side. He perceived her change of attitude and probably thought she was hallucinating.

"Is this your first time here?" He asked.

Even if she was delighted that he decided to speak to her, she kept her eyes a little longer on these perfect images, then confirmed,

"Yes, it is my first time. These images are really amazing. What is it?" she asked as her gaze was back looking at the TV screen.

"It's Discovery Channel," Alexandre replied in a rather amused tone.

"I have never seen this channel before! The images are incredibly beautiful!"

Then Brandon appeared at the entrance of the dining/living room. Happy to see him, and full of energy, Laurie immediately reached out to him. On their way to the room, she was thrilled to have again travelled into space, and undeniably been able to appreciate the incredible view of Earth and the nearby planets. She believed that the Discovery Channel was the reason why she had achieved this feat. Enthusiastically, she told her boyfriend how much she would love to have that channel at home. A little unsettled about her words, Brandon changed the subject and asked what her day had been like.

Once seated on her bed, Laurie lowered her voice, "The Chinese have found me. I saw them today. They put a sensor in my room." Laurie had no filter and didn't wonder how Brandon would perceive her words. On the other hand, she was careful not to tell him where the device was hidden, in case he wanted it to be removed!

Brandon remained quiet. Changing the subject, "There has been a miracle here since I arrived." She wanted him to know about the exceptional event that happened in the dining room, but as a distraction, Brandon asked her to show him around. Not offended, Laurie jumped on her feet, happy as a little girl, and showed him the way.

They headed to the dining room, but once they were both in the corridor, the entire energy around her changed... The corridor illuminated with a pure white light, and again, there was neither a roof nor walls—they had disappeared. Delighted by this magic, Laurie was pleased to walk side by side with Brandon. She grabbed his arm to slow him down, believing they needed to be serious in this physical world as if greater beings were looking at them. In the vision that was becoming more precise, Brandon appeared to be wearing a king's crown, and he was dressed in a large red cape with the edges adorned in silky white fur. Only now did she remember Brandon sacrificed himself on the cross a few days ago, and thought it was a connection. Laurie couldn't see how she was dressed, but for a brief moment, the corridor turned into a grand magnificent golden room. These mixed magic effects provided a sacred atmosphere as if together they would be able to heal everyone on this floor just by walking side by side while reaching the end of the corridor and praying for all the sick.

While Laurie was living this incredible moment, Brandon was following the slow speed of Laurie's steps. Brandon, who had always stayed in the physical world, smiled back at Laurie when she smiled at him. He stopped with her when she stopped, and a few times, he guided by pushing her to move forward when she stopped for too long. Laurie continued to provide prayers until they reached the end of the corridor. "Wow! It was a nice sacred walk, wasn't it?" The vision faded as the real walls reappeared. Without any response from Brandon, she asked him if he would like to visit the big room where they eat or watch tv. Without hesitation, he agreed.

Alexandre and another man were seated on the two sofas and were watching television. The boy with dark hair was alone playing chess in the same place where he usually ate. From the look he gave Laurie this time, he didn't seem happy that she was with someone. *Maybe out of jealousy because he had no visitors?* Nevertheless, she smiled friendly at him, trying to offer him comfort.

In a low toned voice, to respect the boys, Laurie guided Brandon to the window. She was curious to see if there was a crowd on the street this time. But nothing! She showed Brandon the stained-glass sticker glued to the window. "I did something really amazing with this today! I'm not sure it means something in this world but in the other world it was grandiose I think!"

Brandon looked at her with a serious and sincere look and said, "I have no doubt about it!" He didn't want to know more. For him, Laurie was lost in madness, and he did not understand why.

Back in the room, a new nurse in her early forties with curly blonde hair entered and in a professional manner told Brandon, "The time for visits is over. It would be nice if you could respect the visiting hours, both for her and for the other patients." She went on to look at Laurie this time, "Miss Lora, here's your sleeping pill." She gave Laurie a cup of water and waited until the patient swallowed them. "I'll be back to see you soon. Good evening, sir."

Brandon hugged his girlfriend hard, feeling sad about the situation. He whispered in her ears, "I love you. I hope you'll rest well. I don't know if I will visit you tomorrow because Angela and Peter would like to come and see you."

"No worries, just come back when you can." Laurie understood he needed time for himself.

Feeling good, Laurie was ready to receive the nurse who sat and settled in such a way as to be comfortable, seeming sincere and willing to listen to her patient's journey.

"My name is Sophie. How was your day, Laurie?"

"I had a good day; I slept a lot. I'm glad my boyfriend came to see me."

Sophie looked at her patient like a friend would.

"Yes, it's important to have good people around for times like these. Your boyfriend looks very nice. He writes books?"

Sophie knew how to start a conversation. Laurie spoke rapidly about the event during the manifestation and how Brandon had crucified himself. Then, she mentioned Christ's story and her desire to help humanity... Sophie was listening until she waved to the roommate to come in the room. Standing up, Sophie thanked Laurie for sharing with her and with emotion, she left with a tear in her eye.

Happy but tired, Laurie thanked the nurse for listening, confessing that it did her a lot of good to be able to free herself. She then wished her roommate a good night, which she returned the favor.

Before Laurie fell asleep, the images of the planets she saw earlier during her out-of-body journey reappeared in her mind. These images were wonderful... But suddenly, without expecting it, she was back in the galaxy. She didn't bother to understand how and why such a phenomenon was happening again. She was there, grateful, admiring the solar system. She experienced gravity and weightlessness again without a need to breathe—a glorious moment of fullness. The image was fantastic, but an emotion of fear began to invade her as she looked at the Earth. *Why?*

The view of the Earth from space made her realize that the Earth was unquestionably standing out. A huge portion of it was covered with yellow light from the abundant electricity light of human consumption. The contrast with the blue color of the oceans and the dazzling lights from human civilization was definite. She had no doubt it was America she was seeing. She could easily depict large cities such as Vancouver, Montreal, New York, Los Angeles, Mexico... She was amazed to witness the perimeter and the massive discharge of lights of each of them. It was incredibly bright. TOO bright! From her location in space, she could feel the energy of human overconsumption. The panic inside her continued as she was also feeling the vibration of all the energies of the telecommunications surrounding Mother Earth.

During this inexplicable moment, in her field of vision to her right, Laurie saw an extraterrestrial being; his head had a triangle-shape. He had a glazed look with big black oval eyes much like a black mirror. Laurie was afraid when she realized his skin color was grey and an extreme panic ran through her body as she understood that it was the little grey men; the terrific unknown that her mother Hetty had talked about when Laurie was a child. Hetty was taking cosmic science classes, and Laurie had heard her mother talking in a low voice with her uncles and aunts about what she had learned, "According to the teacher, possibly one day our humanity would be destroyed by an invasion of grey men that would come from another galaxy."

Laurie was aware that some people were incredulous. But she was also aware that others were afraid it may happen. Since her childhood and as she grew older, she had heard about the grey men and every time, she immediately had goosebumps all over her body.

As Laurie looked at the vision of the alien's physical body, she wondered why she was seeing him. Then suddenly, he moved his eyes and looked towards her. The facial expression of the extraterrestrial changed; wrinkles in his forehead had been formed and the expression of surprise appeared on his face when he opened his mouth like saying, "O."

Laurie was frightened because that story was apparently true! She was scared because she felt he had seen her but then, she was terrified because it wasn't about her. It was about the Earth! *He sees our planet like I see it!* Laurie understood that the surprise on his face was because he had just discovered our world. And it was due to the excess of light and the emanation of energy from telecommunications that he had seen our globe from so far away. Feeling terrified because she felt he was attracted to our planet, and petrified of the thought his colony would want to invade us. She felt like they had used all their resources in their galaxy, and they were trying to find another place to survive.

His expression seeming to say "O" gave Laurie the impression that he saw an easy way to reach out to this enticing planet... that thought immensely scared her. She was petrified this could happen. *But how could it be?*

Laurie's heart skipped a beat. Tears were flowing down her physical body while her consciousness was propelled even further into space to be a witness to something else. A "click" had resonated. It was the same kind of click that she had felt a few days ago, but before knowing more, she had fainted. This time, with the panoramic view of all the planets almost aligned in the galaxy, her understanding about the "click" was to announce the complete alignment of all the planets of the solar system.

With the many theories heard in the past about the end of the world in 2012: the alignment of the planets, the end of the Maya calendar and what she was experiencing now, Laurie was shocked as she realized that everything was connected. *The process had begun!* Maybe it was the grey man's vision she saw... but Laurie was seeing a colony of unknown crossing into our galaxy. With the phenomena of the alignment of planets, she saw a spaceship traveling and using the energetic traction of each planet of the solar system, and it simply went straight ahead towards the desirable illuminated planet.

Perhaps because Laurie was afraid to be seen from the grey man, or maybe she had seen enough of what she needed to see, instantly she returned to her body.

Laurie was back in the hospital bed. She sincerely believed the alien had found the human world and that one day soon, he and his colony would arrive and invade it. Laurie began to pray to God and Mary asking for protection. Crying silently, she imagined a huge black shield that would hide the Earth and the entire solar system from their sight. Even more, she hoped that all the electricity and the telecommunicate energy would shut down so they wouldn't be able to find this unique place, and eventually they would just give up their search.

Still in panic, she wondered what more she could do. Then the image of the Maya calendar appeared before her eyes. As if to show the connection between the line-up of the planets and the end of the world that scientists had talked about.

Finally, and fortunately for Laurie, the pill had taken effect. She fell asleep without worrying about anything anymore.

~ 17 ~

The Grey Alien

The two roommates finally met in the morning. With a friendly smile, Laurie asked her name. "Seasol," she said, seemingly embarrassed. While Laurie remained silent because something was jostling in her head, the roommate repeated, seemingly irritated, "Seasol... like the fertilizer."

Laurie had never heard of someone named like that and she loved it. "'Sea' like in English for 'Ocean' and 'Sol' like in Spanish for 'Sun'! Ocean-Sun. I love it!" Seasol understood what her new roommate meant, and she smiled as if her entire being had just woken up with happiness. Laurie was thrilled that her kind words had such a positive effect on her roommate. She was grateful to her friend Diego who had taught her Spanish during her vacation in Hawaii.

The two girls began to chat, and Laurie began to have a sense of immensity. She felt as if she could predict everything Seasol was about to say before she even spoke. The scenery around them began to change, and Laurie was in admiration looking at a vast, dry, and wild terrain. She had a vision of Africa even before Seasol told her it was her birth country and how she missed it tremendously. As she was listening to her new friend talking about her journey that brought her to the hospital, Laurie was feeling the breeze of this foreign country. She was enchanted and stunned at the same time, because she could see a giraffe and an elephant at about fifty feet away from them. The two magnificent animals were walking slowly in her direction, while stopping for a moment to eat food from a few trees. Laurie wondered if those gigantic wonders could see her. Unsure, she kept the vision to herself.

"Wow, Africa must be beautiful! I am fascinated by this continent. Is it more of a dry continent?"

"It depends on the location. Where I lived, it was often the rainy season!"

"Have you ever seen giraffes and elephants?" Laurie asked in haste.

Seasol smiled with her sparkling eyes, as she reminded herself of wonderful memories, but she had to keep her thoughts to herself as Dr. Dion entered the room, asking her if she could leave them alone for a moment. Dr. Dion needed time to talk with Laurie.

Appearing to be in a hurry, Dr. Dion inquired how Laurie was doing and if she was sleeping well at night. Disappointed to be back in the hospital room décor and to have lost the sense of immensity, Laurie answered briefly as she preferred to meet the others for breakfast.

Laurie wasted no time and headed to the dining room. Everyone was already seated, and she noticed Seasol at the second table signaling her to join her. The two new friends chatted over breakfast. Laurie felt normal as nothing unusual had occurred. Patients around were also chatting and laughing with the discrete supervision of nurse Sophie, who was sitting on the rocking chair outside in the hallway.

Back in their room, authorized to go outside, Seasol grabbed her backpack and left. Laurie grabbed the book that Brandon had brought her and went to sit with the others at the end of the corridor.

Sitting in the same chair on the left, Laurie was looking at the room in front of her. All she could see was a nurse sitting on a chair at the foot of the bed. Laurie wondered who this patient could be. Seconds later, she had a vision of a young man, positioned in the shape of a fetus, all curled up, unable to pronounce a word clearly. Curious, she frowned trying to understand this disease.

Another vision appeared; in front of her, a child of about five-years-old was looking at her with a partial smile. He had a beautiful face and was dressed like the man he stood next to. He was so small that his head barely reached the man's hips. This adorable child's posture was slightly bent to the right side. Oddly, Laurie viewed this image in black and white as to suggest it was an old disease. And the way the dad, perhaps, took the little boy's hand with authority and impatience and quickly left the place, gave the impression the mom had passed away.

What Laurie understood from this vision was that the man had never accepted the imperfection of his son, and he wanted to place his child at perhaps a boarding school. *Rejection, abandonment, and lack of love were surely the reason the patient's body had physically closed on himself,* Laurie thought.

Believing in that vision, she was sad for the patient. Laurie opened her book to the first page and asked the Lord and Mary to embrace the patient in their divine light, to love him and to heal him. A few tears fell on the pages of her book. Unable to concentrate on her reading, but to appear credible she was reading, Laurie slowly turned the pages of her book until the patient began to fidget in his room.

Laurie discreetly wiped her tears off the paper and off her face, and then watched the nurse move to this patient who was creating sounds that resembled laughter or cries of joy. The three other men rocking on their chairs next to Laurie, were now looking at her, craving for gossip. But Laurie signaled to them that she couldn't see what was going on. Some seemed happy and surprised to hear him laughing. *Great, the prayer certainly worked!* As to validate her thought, she asked the men if the patient often laughed like that.

One old man said, "First time I heard him laugh."

A second man said, "Usually the door is closed."

The third man did not appear to have followed the discussion and was rocking his chair at a rapid pace. Laurie approached them and introduced herself.

"Hello, my name is Laurie."

"Nice to meet you. My name is Mathieu. He's Félix and he's Wilfred."

"Delighted," she told them as she sat back on her chair, continuing to pretend to be reading.

Just after dinner, Laurie barely had time to sit down to watch the news as a nurse arrived, and asked Laurie if she had read the brochure guide that recommended resting in her room after meals. Surprised and with the desire to do the right thing, Laurie answered her, "Yes, the guide to live in psychiatry?" The brochure had been placed on the side of the window, and Laurie had taken a long time in the afternoon to read it because she couldn't concentrate like she used to. "I read it all and I don't think it was talking about naps." Laurie said now feeling unsure.

The nurse seemed to have calmed down as she was trying to remember if the guide was mentioning it, but finally reminded her patient,

"It would be nice if after every meal you would rest in your room."

"Okay, how long do I need to rest?" Laurie kindly asked.

The nurse hesitated for a moment, then went on,

"As long as you manage to fall asleep."

Laurie sensed the nurse wanted the best for her and she was grateful for it. Pleased with that discussion, Laurie went to her room. It was daylight and she had to make a conscious effort to set aside all the thoughts that were running through her mind, and finally fell asleep.

Laurie woke up feeling well-rested, pleased with herself because she had managed to take a nap, and with an abounding amount of happiness because her Godmother Angela and Godfather Peter were there to visit her, both smiling at her. *What a great reward!* She thought as she appreciably sensed an incredible phenomenon of their great love surrounding and comforting her.

Enjoying this moment, Laurie stood up immediately and greeted them. Angela was dressed somewhat different than usual. Or maybe it was the fantasy Laurie had back in her mind. Peter and Laurie stood by the window while Angela, who was dressed in a sweatshirt, cowboy style, leaned on the bed, put her hands on the mattress and gave herself a gentle push to finally find a comfortable sitting position. Angela seemed happy about her performance and began to swing her legs in the empty space in front of her. Laurie burst out laughing at the image because she saw another image at the same time. Instantly Angela and Peter laughed heartily with her, and then Angela asked,

"Why do you laugh?"

"I just had a vision while you sat down. You were a little girl seemingly to be at Grandpa's farm, and you sat on the hay bales giving a push just like you did here. You had the same jovial look as you succeed with your jump and finding a comfortable position."

Laurie shared with them as if they could understand.

"It was strange, but pleasant to see!"

Curious, Angela looked at her goddaughter for a moment and then said,

"Laurie, it's weird what's happening to you!"

"I know. It's like I'm super open. As if my mind travels back in time. I see things that I couldn't see before."

Laurie tried to show them, with the help of her hands, that all around her head, there was no barrier, no fences blocking her mind. Unfortunately, they didn't seem to understand what had become Laurie's reality. Unsure what to respond, Angela and Peter kept quiet. Because Laurie wanted to be one hundred percent honest with them, she added, "These visions don't appear all the time! And I don't know why I see them!" Again, they remained silent. To change the subject, Laurie asked them if they wanted to go and take a tour of the hospital floor. They both agreed.

As the three of them began to walk down the corridor, the narrow walls and ceiling disappeared again and only Laurie could admire the sky above dotted with stars, and they were walking on an unfamiliar ground-like sand. She didn't wonder if it was rational or not. She was just at peace sensing they were walking as if they were the three kings going to meet Jesus. When they arrived at the end of the long corridor, impulsively, Laurie pointed at the last room to the right and told Angela and Peter, "The Messiah is in this room." Unsure what she was supposed to do next, she waited to see what they would do, but they didn't seem to understand the situation. The present-time décor gradually reappeared, and finally Laurie led her visitors to the big room.

They sat alone at the second table. Laurie asked them how work was going. Peter was more than happy that she asked since he had a few important questions regarding some passwords and what needed to be done urgently. Laurie was the only one controlling the office tasks for the last year or so. Fortunately, she remembered all the passwords and wrote them down on a piece of paper, she answered their questions, and let them know what needed attending to and what needed to be paid. Relieved to have their questions answered, both seemed happily surprised to have re-connected with the person Laurie had always been—professional and interested in her work.

Back to the room, just before Angela and Peter were about to leave, for the first time, Laurie remembered the vision she had last night about the grey man and felt the necessity to tell them. She had a serious look when she asked,

"You took cosmic science classes with my mother, right?"

Angela looked intrigued and said, "Yes."

Peter seemed equally intrigued.

"In these classes, you were talking about the little grey men, weren't you? I've heard my mother talking about this topic with other adults when I was a child."

Without realizing it, Angela looked up as she was thinking. She then smiled remembering the information they had learned in this class. Laurie didn't want to laugh about it as it was too serious and too dangerous to take lightly—the present situation deserved to be taken seriously.

"I saw one grey man last night. An alien from another galaxy found us!"

After a few seconds, Uncle Peter asked what she meant. Laurie answered with anxiety in her voice, "Because of the over-consumption of energy that we use here on earth, they found our planet!"

They listened attentively to what their goddaughter was trying to explain to them. Above all, they wanted to understand what was happening to her. Laurie interpreted their gaze as if they were saying, *Tell us more.* Then, Laurie had the impression Aunt Angela's soul had awoken and had taken control. It was as if an inner presence was surrounding her aunt and was looking directly at Laurie, eager to find out if she had discovered the mystery that was happening in another dimension.

Feeling she was taken seriously, she revisited last night's vision and explained, "The complete alignment of the planets has begun, and the grey man will take advantage of this phenomenon to easily reach the earth, using the traction from planet to planet, it would be so easy for them to travel to us."

Peter and Angela had already heard about these stories in their classes but didn't know what to say. Standing beside her, they were silent. With tears in her eyes, Laurie was sincerely sad and frightened. She continued thinking she was still addressing their higher being,

"I'm afraid that not too long from now, we'll see several spaceships flying around taking over our Earth and our Galaxy."

"Well, don't worry Laurie." Angela said while hugging her goddaughter.

Laurie had to take a break to calm down. She wanted to find the right words and to share with them the connection that had become so clear to her.

"But you don't understand! The Mayan calendar ends exactly when the planets are perfectly aligned. The Mayan probably knew that another species could try to use this phenomenon to enter our galaxy. And now, with the over-consumption of electricity and telecommunications all around the Earth, it's like we're rolling out the red carpet to them so they can reach us directly. And why is 2012 the last year of the Mayan calendar? And why do some people say 2012 is the end of the world?"

Laurie was back in her aunt's arms, looking at her uncle's sad eyes when the nurse arrived and asked if everything was okay.

Wanting to protect her niece, Angela replied,

"Yes, I think she's just tired."

She held Laurie longer in her arms and told her,

"I assure you Laurie, this will not happen."

While listening to those words, Laurie had the feeling that the answer came directly from her aunt's inner being and she might be right.

Angela and Peter were shaken when they left. The nurse gave Laurie's medication and asked about her day, but Laurie was brief as she'd rather be alone.

On the bed, Laurie recalled what she had said to her godmother and godfather. Then without seeing it coming, her spirit was back into the galaxy, looking at the Earth and the planets. The grey men reappeared. She pushed him away just like she had done to the dog that barked in the deep of her mind on Monday night. Physically she used her right hand to push it away.

Mysteriously, the same pale brown type of Pitbull reappeared and was again aggressively coming at her. When Laurie tried to push him out of her mind, he immediately grew bigger as she watched this beast jump from nowhere onto Planet Earth. Laurie found this phenomenon extremely bizarre and then everything froze on an image. Time had stopped and she didn't understand what she was witnessing in the moment. The dog was as large as the Planet Earth and he was sitting on it, covering the entire American continent. His head and upper body covered the expanse of Canada, while his back and hind legs covered the United States, his buttocks and tail covered South America.

While Laurie waited to see what would happen next, on the far right, at the end of the planetary alignment, the grey alien began to activate and move towards the Earth. Immediately, the Pitbull leaped into space, disappearing leaving behind the Planet Earth, turning on itself due to its massive jump. This phenomenon vibrated throughout the alignment. Surprised, Laurie searched for the spaceships, but they seemed to have deviated from their trajectories. Because she couldn't see them, she felt relieved believing they were lost in the vastness of our galaxy.

She looked upon the Earth that had almost stopped spinning. The lights and telecommunications had gone out, resembling that of a ghost planet. Laurie was worried, *What had become of the globe and the people?* Seconds later, strangely she felt reassured by the light of the moon. She began to admire this light that oddly seemed to illuminate mainly the east and west coast of the United States. Laurie took a better look and realized the light was illuminating the traces left by the push of the Pitbulls' hind legs as he jumped in space. His monstrous push had shaken part of San Francisco and Manhattan Island in New York.

Laurie's spirit returned to her body. Shaken by that vision, she remembered the predictions of the San Andreas Fault in California and the engulfment of Manhattan. She thought the prophesies predicted by Nostradamus had just taken place! She felt so sad, and at the same time relief the Earth was safe from the grey men. Laurie prayed for the people of New York and San Francisco as she questioned that unbelievable vision. Then the medication put an end to her questioning and finally, Laurie went into a deep sleep for the night.

~ 18 ~

Sorceresses (healers)

Brandon arrived early that morning as he wanted to be present for Laurie's meeting with the doctor. He had talked last night with Angela and Peter about their last visit, and he was furious to hear what they had told him. Brandon reported to the doctor's office about what his girlfriend was talking about, and Dr. Dion suggested Laurie's medication probably wasn't strong enough.

While walking together in the hallway, spontaneously, Laurie asked Brandon if he had heard anything special that happened on Earth last night. Brandon seemed intrigued due to the concerned look on Laurie's face.

"Why?" He asked.

"You should look at the international news when you have a chance. I think New York and San Francisco sank into the ocean last night."

Then Laurie looked at Brandon rushing to the nurse's counter to find out what time the doctor would meet with them.

Laurie reached him but got distracted with the *Montreal newspapers* on the left side of the counter. Brandon was waiting for an answer while Laurie was curious if the news reported anything about last night's phenomenon. There was no headline related to the catastrophe of her vision, so she simply continued turning the pages thinking the news would mention this topic later on the TV or the radio. When she got to the obituary pages, she had a strange feeling she was able to see the souls of deceased people coming out freely from the newspaper and reaching the sky above. Unsure whether it was possible, she looked at Brandon, but he was gone and already in the room.

Dr. Dion and Brandon were talking when Laurie entered smiling, and with a feeling of confidence. Brandon walked in circles within the small space, seemingly nervous and angry. Dr. Dion was quite calm and began telling her patient, "Laurie, we think we should increase the dosage of your medication."

"Ah, it's funny that you're talking about it, I wanted to start decreasing it."

Laurie had responded faster than her thoughts. She was surprised they were talking about increasing her dosage, since she was sleeping well at night.

Brandon was about to explode with frustration as he was looking at the doctor who continued, "We find that it is far too early to lower your dose. It can be dangerous for you."

But Laurie remained calm and confident.

"Since I arrived here, I sleep well, I eat well, and I am listening well to the nurses' instructions. I'm ready to decrease my medication."

Brandon and Dr. Dion signaled to each other that they didn't agree with decreasing the medication. Laurie was becoming upset. *How can they judge me? They barely saw me lately!*

"I'm telling you. I don't want to increase my medication," she firmly said.

"So, we're going to continue your dose as it is now. Is that okay with you Miss Lora?" the doctor asked realizing Laurie's change in mood.

"I'm fine with it, but soon we're going to reduce the dose," Laurie answered with a slight irritable tone. *It's my body and my mind after all!*

Unhappy about that decision, Brandon left at the same time as the doctor. Not bothered, proud to stand up for herself, Laurie took her book and went to sit at the end of the corridor.

The same three men were rocking on their chair while Laurie was sending good prayers to the patient in the next room. Mr. Mathieu, the old man who Laurie sat next to, leaned in close to her and said, "There's a lot going on here. They lock me up and they don't want to tell me why."

Laurie waited for him to continue his statement, but he stayed silent, and leaned back on his chair when he saw a nurse arriving. He seemed worried as his teeth clenched. Laurie discreetly placed her hand on his knee, trying to reassure him. He looked at her and nodded that he was okay, but he didn't convince Laurie.

The nurse sat next to Wilfred and started to ask him strange questions in front of everyone. Laurie found her manners indiscreet and unprofessional. She recalled having the same feeling about the nurse, the night before, for making another patient have the same uneasy feeling. *Why?* Slowly, it became clear to Laurie the nurse has this need to show authority and power over the patients. *Her behavior of a power trip is not good for the patient! She doesn't have the right job!* Wanting to remain positive, Laurie started to imagine pure light surrounding all of them sitting at the end of the corridor. A moment later, the nurse seemed to be tired and left in the middle of a discussion, without saying a word to anybody.

Everyone watched the nurse leave. Laurie looked back at the men and noticed Félix, who was sitting between the two men, didn't seem to feel good. He was chewing his gum fast, looking straight ahead, seeming unable to relax and breath well. *He's going to lose it if he doesn't relax a little!* To help him, Laurie imagined expanding his etheric space at the level of his chest to help him breathe. Immediately, she observed him calm down. He was chewing his gum and rocking his chair at a much slower pace. Like the two other men, he seemed to wonder what had just happened to him.

Pleased by this great accomplishment, Laurie remembered a similar and previous phenomenon that she had experienced with her good friend Isabelle a few years prior. It was the reason for her beliefs in this kind of healing.

Isabelle had a bad time, unfortunately, everything was falling apart in her life. Laurie had invited Isabelle to come to her house and stay for the night, telling her she would take care of her. Distressed, Isabelle gratefully accepted. Before she arrived, Laurie had prayed to Mary and asked her angels to heal her friend Isabelle... At about 4:30 in the morning, Isabelle was getting ready for work. Because of the light in the hallway, Laurie woke up and saw Isabelle about to enter the bathroom. Before entering the room, Isabelle had stopped in the door frame and amazingly, Laurie noticed a second source of light was surrounding her friend. Laurie looked more carefully at the phenomenon that was taking form. Then, as if by magic, Laurie saw two angels on each side of Isabelle's back, at the height of her shoulder blades. Each one was about the size of a small hummingbird and they were pulling on their opposite sides to open more of her etheric body as to help her breathe better. Hypnotized, Laurie understood that her friend Isabelle's body wasn't taking enough time to breathe, like she was worrying more about others then herself. Moved about what she saw, Laurie was grateful that her prayer had been heard, and even more so, for the privilege of seeing these two little angels in action. Then Isabelle closed the door behind, and Laurie fell asleep, convinced her friend would feel better now. Two days later, noticing Isabelle was suddenly feeling better emotionally, Naomi, a common friend, had mentioned to Isabelle, "You probably went to see Laurie!"

While Mr. Mathieu started talking again to the people around, Laurie was looking at the tall guy who she had been intrigued with the day before; he was surrounded with people helping him walk, sit, and clean his dripping mouth, but this time, he was weakly coming alone. He sat with difficulty on a chair in front of Laurie. Curious, staring at him, Laurie wondered what his issue could be. Félix surprised her as he talked to Laurie for the first time. He pointed to the tall guy,

"His name is Sébastien, and he is in this state because of the treatment he had received yesterday. The doctors gave him electric shocks."

With his hands, he showed the area of the temples where he received the shocks, as if it was nothing.

"What?"

Laurie was outraged. She remembered the story of a famous Canadian singer who had received lobotomy against her will. Since that story, Laurie always thought this barbaric procedure had been banned. She looked and smiled at Sébastien who was in front of her, and asked Mother Mary to surround him with her divine light, her healing, and her love. Sébastien was bipolar and she wanted him to find a way to adjust his mood changes himself so he could avoid these brutal treatments, in her opinion.

Laurie opened her book to the first page. Many times, she had to read the same sentence to understand the meaning. The door next to the room in front of her slowly opened and Laurie began to be distracted by the movement. In the room, there was an old lady in a blue hospital robe standing in front of the door frame. Laurie remembered seeing her once, alone in her room changing her voice while brushing her long white hair. Laurie had thought the lady suffered from Alzheimer, and her mind was back in her childhood, pretending with her sweet voice playing the role of a princess, then with a mad voice, playing the role of a wicked sorceress. Even if it was totally crazy, immediately Laurie had felt affection for her and continued while looking at that lady, now speaking out loud, seemingly trying to encourage herself to cross the floor line between her room and the corridor. When the lady finally managed to cross the corridor, she was smiling so proudly that Laurie thought she had crossed into another world. While the old lady looked both ways trying to make a decision which side she was going to take, Sophie, the nurse, passed by her side and greeted her, "Hello Mrs. Esther," but the old lady waved her hand at the nurse seeming to say, *Don't bother me!* It was obvious that she did not want to talk.

Fascinated by her behavior, Laurie was looking at Mrs. Esther coming her way. The lady stopped next to her, stood while looking at the threshold that separated the corridor and the dining room behind Laurie. Seemingly confronted again with another invisible line, the lady began to stomp her feet and was talking loudly for about thirty seconds before she managed to pass from Laurie's field of vision.

All patients were quiet and Laurie was discretely smiling as she thought of this lady, who's body seemed to be similar to the pictures of history that represented witches; an old body bent forward, a white skin with deep wrinkles, as well as a pronounced nose. Laurie was wondering the possibility Mrs. Esther had once been a witch. Then she felt the air around changing; the décor opened onto a starry black sky, there were no more walls or ceilings, and some grey clouds appeared. Laurie's spirit seemed to be floating among the clouds, because as she was a bird, she saw few people on Earth moving around a fire. The light from the full moon intensified, and her spirit was gazing while descending slowly on the Earth. She saw few people; women she thought, dancing around a fire. Without knowing more about this vision, the phenomenon ended. Laurie's spirit was back among many other patients who were receiving their trays of food for dinner.

Dinner and a nap had passed. Laurie quickly went to the large room and sat on the sofa, next to Alexandre. Watching TV, she was hoping to find out what had happened to the Earth, the planets, and the space with the spaceships, according to her vision from last night.

Mrs. Esther, the old lady, eventually approached quietly close to Alexandre and Laurie who had all their attention on the TV. Oddly, there was more information scrolling at the bottom of the screen and it was like Laurie was seeing it for the first time. She believed it was especially for her, so she paid more attention while wondering if Alexandre could read it, too. The written news was about the Quebec prime minister and the student protest.

The old lady was in her own world still standing next to Laurie who was waiting to see images of planets that never came. Laurie's subconscious told her, *You will not see the planet again. The last time, the Higher Beings managed to make you see it because they wanted to draw your attention to an extraordinary phenomenon.* Believing it was possible, Laurie was amazed and impressed. Enthusiastically she turned to Mrs. Esther who was deep in her thoughts, still standing up and slightly off balance. Laurie was looking forward to talking with her, wanting to know her story, and where she came from... Mrs. Esther's lips were moving, and her mind was far away when Laurie disturbed her soul saying, "Hello Mrs. Esther."

The old lady shook her head, seeming to wonder who was bothering her. Laurie noticed her behavior changed when she looked at her, then at

Alexandre, and then came back to Laurie.

"What do you want?" she said upset with her right hand already making a gesture to Laurie that seemed to say, *Get out of the way!*

Not offended, trying to cross the veil between them, Laurie said,

"I just wanted to say hello to you."

But Mrs. Esther didn't reply–she was back in her thoughts.

"I think it's because she wants to sit next to me." Alexandre explained, "I don't know why, but it seemed like she's nice only with me. As if she thinks I'm her boyfriend."

Alexandre then looked at Mrs. Esther and said, raising his voice enough so she might hear him well,

"Esther, she is my friend, Laurie, and she can sit here."

But Mrs. Esther stared at Laurie and articulated well,

"Little bitch."

Laurie immediately and silently cracked up to hear an old lady saying these words–*But she seemed to be a sweet woman inside! Why does she want to scare people away?* Following her questioning, an image of Mrs. Esther appeared; she was young with long blond hair, dressed in a beige dress. She was working outside, surrounded by plants, herbs and spices, exuding happiness, and kindness. In Laurie's vision, people were coming to her because she knew how to cure diseases with herbal remedies from nature. The idea that came with the vision was "*witches,*" confirming Mrs. Esther was a healer (witch) earlier in this life, or in another life.

Probably because of seeing Mrs. Esther at a young age, a mental connection in Laurie's mind was created with her good fifty-year-old spiritual friend Lisa, who also had the same facial features as Mrs. Esther. Laurie often thought of Lisa having an old spirit related to sorcerers. (Lisa was the friend who had given great advice to Laurie when she was seeing barbarism from another era. She had suggested looking at the visions without judgments, and to let them flow in and out. Those scary visions had never returned because Laurie had accepted that they were memories from a passed life.)

As Laurie realized that those two ladies had the same open mind on mystical subjects, she began to believe they were sorceresses together in a previous life. And as she accepted this possibility, the vision Laurie had an hour ago reappeared. The décor reopened into a starry black sky, but she could see the people closer. Among ladies dancing around a fire, dressed in beige clothes, Laurie saw herself; she was the youngest one and weirdly, because of the shape of her rolled-up nose, she sensed she was a sorcerer's apprentice. *This is why I have all these visions! My soul had lived in that time, and I had kept skills and memories of those days.* Convinced, Laurie felt she had just found her true self and was happy thinking to have been a mystical healer's apprentice.

The vision continued. There were men walking with determined steps and fire torches in their hands. Due to the men's clothing, it seemed to Laurie the vision was from centuries ago. Deep in her vision, Laurie could feel their need for power and control. They sought to destroy those sorceresses. At one moment, it felt like Laurie was revisiting her own memories from a past life. There was an image of a wooden platform, with women on it, fighting and screaming before they were hung and burned. They had been called "witches" by the ones who had empowered themselves wrongly to execute someone else, but also, by the cowardly and ignorant who wouldn't do anything to halt this stupidity; Laurie included. She was not innocent because she did nothing to stop the massacre; not understanding at the time what was happening due to her young age.

Sad, she got up and offered her chair to Mrs. Esther, who looked at Laurie with a different expression on her face, as if she had also witnessed the same vision.

Laurie went to sit on a chair behind them and a new powerful vision overtook Laurie's complete attention. In her mind, she saw the bright Sun approaching in a marvelous way, slowly, very close to the Earth. Arriving from the Sun, she saw the body of a man emerging from this light, who magically began to walk on the Earth. He already had the physical body of a man in his thirties, surrounded by a pure and powerful light. Laurie was stunned when she thought this was the way Jesus had come to the Earth. At the same time, something higher whispered in her mind, *This is also what some men did to this child of light when he came to teach us, help us, and love us. Those frightened and greedy men, with their need of power, had burned the witches just like they had crucified Jesus before.*

Laurie's full consciousness came back into the room among the other patients. She was troubled by those memories and the considerable impact it had on the human species. She was even more saddened to realize that still today, there was this type of person on Earth—people who think (wrongly) that they own people's lives.

Laurie was looking at the screen on the TV, but her mind was trying to understand the visions that just appeared to her... the Sun, then a being of light coming out and coming to Earth. Laurie could see Him again. She could almost touch the being of light who transformed and had appeared in a physical form. *It was Jesus!? It all made sense!* As Laurie accepted the idea, the word "Trinity" came to her mind suggesting; *The Sun is the father, the Earth is the mother, and together they created another life; Jesus's physical body.*

Laurie was amazed with the discovery and her understanding. As if they had shared the same vision, Mrs. Esther got up, she turned and looked directly at Laurie with her beautiful piercing blue eyes, and magnificent smile even though she was missing a few teeth. Then she left the place peacefully.

A few minutes later, Alexandre and Laurie were about to leave, when a nurse entered the room. She stopped Laurie, and quickly handed her medication with a plastic glass half filled with water, and then left right away saying, "I will meet you in your room in a little bit."

When Laurie put the pill on her tongue, she immediately felt the pill heavier than the previous ones. Without thinking too much, she took the pill out of her mouth, looked around to find a tissue, and carefully covered the pill.

Exhausted, Laurie went to bed and fell asleep easily, but around

3:00 a.m., for the first time since her arrival, she became aware that a nurse was in her room with her flashlight, looking to see if the patient was sleeping. Laurie moved by reflex due to the light that blinded her. An hour later, the nurse entered again, and Laurie's reflex was the same. The nurse came up close and asked Laurie in a soft and low voice,

"Would you like to have a pill that would help you sleep?"

"No thank you. I don't know why I'm not sleeping. But I'm sure I'll be soon."

Kind and calm, the nurse spontaneously said,

"I also don't understand why you don't sleep, because your dose had been increased."

"Are you sure of that?" Laurie asked, surprised, remembering the agreement in the morning with the doctor, to keep the same dose.

"Yes, it was written in the file that today was the new dosage given to you."

The nurse left and Laurie found it exceptional that she had sensed the weight difference of a few milligrams with the new medication on her tongue. She also found it weird the nurse who gave her the pill had not taken the time to verify if she swallowed it. Laurie then wondered which master helped her in this crucial moment to not take a stronger medication. *My Grandmother? God? My soul?*

But Laurie did not receive any answer. Before falling asleep, she silently thanked the young nurse with the flashlight for being honest with her.

***

In days to come, Laurie's visions will diminish in quantities and intensity as well as her need to pray to Mother Mary. Slowly coming back to the reality of the physical world, Laurie's idea of a spiritual parallel dimension will fade as well.

~ 19 ~

Helping Other Patients

Many patients were waiting for breakfast at the end of the corridor. Laurie imagined sending healing energy to the patient in the next room. She listened to Mr. Mathieu talking about where he was from and conversed about the regions he had visited. Without a warning, Laurie's mind began to fly over the central portion of Quebec. With a fantasy effect, she could see the Appalachian Mountains and the towns they had talked about—she saw the lakes, the rivers, the roads, the houses.

Laurie's vision stopped when a nurse exited the room in front of her with the patient in a wheelchair. Silence consumed the immediate area, *Is it the first time that others are seeing him?* Everyone was looking at the patient whose arms and feet were bent inward, and his head would have been much more arched forward if it had not been for the belt strapped to his forehead. To see him uncomfortably curled up reinforced Laurie's earlier vision of him in a fetal position to be accurate.

She wanted to make him feel accepted, so she asked what his name was. The nurse stopped close to Laurie seeming to feel relief that someone was interested and said, "His name is Pascal." Restricted due to his disability, Pascal was trying to look up at Laurie and the others. "Nice to meet you, Pascal." Laurie said. Seasol had just joined the group and greeted him too. Then they all greeted him. Pascal became agitated in his chair, so the nurse took him back to his room and closed the door. Laurie believed that throughout his debilitating disease, Pascal had developed a sixth sense, and he was able to hear and to feel what others could not. So, she tried to send him good vibrations. *Be strong Pascal. Hope I'll see you soon.*

Further down the hall, Mrs. Rita, a lady in her early fifties, dressed in a blue hospital robe was walking with difficulty towards the group. Everyone could tell she was in pain; her arms as well as her legs were red and swollen with large black and blue marks. As she was wondering what the lady's situation was, Laurie understood she was receiving treatment for her skin and for anxiety. *But are the swollen areas due to a bad medication? If so, are doctors going to increase or decrease her dosage?* The lady's salt and pepper hair fell on her shoulders and hid most of her face. And behind her oversized square black glasses, Laurie perceived how much the lady was sad and anxious. Laurie felt Mrs. Rita's heart was beating so fast that she presumed she was going to collapse at any time. Without hesitation, she reached her and helped her sit down on the first chair on the left. During this maneuver, Laurie felt Mrs. Rita trembling hands, and heard the despair in her voice.

Proud for her good action, Laurie returned her book to her room before breakfast. As she walked straight in the middle of the corridor, holding her book with both hands outstretched at the height of her belly, she felt confident and walked with a little swing in her step, happy that no one would judge her.

Halfway, Laurie was about to meet the black-haired 'mean' boy. She sensed that he was a decent and sensitive person, but internally, he was fighting against something negative and dark. She wanted to help him, and strangely, she felt that he could be a brother from another life. She stopped him quite spontaneously and asked his name. A part of him seemed to want to tell her, *It's none of her business*! but another part of him seemed to be surprised she wanted to know. With a suspicious attitude he responded, "Dominic." Before continuing on her way. Laurie smiled, satisfied thinking she had awakened his curiosity.

There were far less people on Saturday afternoon. Laurie was sitting at the end of the corridor with the three same men rocking in their chairs and three other ladies who were talking quietly. Sébastien, the tall man who had received electroshock treatments, sat next to Laurie. He was dressed quite differently, wearing a pair of jeans and a white T-shirt. He mumbled and no one seemed to understand him. His head was leaning forward, his chin was touching his chest, and his back was bent due to his poor positioning on his chair. He tried to tell Laurie something, but she couldn't understand him. He was looking at the floor and was talking with a low tone of voice that lacked energy. Impulsively, Laurie sat straight up in her chair. She looked towards him and emphasized her pronunciation and with a slight smile asked him, "What are you saying?"

The tall man imitated her right away. He also sat straight up, looked at Laurie, and he began to speak clearly, "What are you reading?" Everyone around seemed amazed and happy for him. For her part, Laurie was very happy to see his change of attitude. He was suddenly more awake with a rapid improvement. *Wow, he has power!* But Laurie rationally began to come back quietly and thought instead; *It's just the posture that makes all the difference!* For a long time, the two new friends easily conversed until he seemed tired and got up to leave for his room.

Soon after, Laurie noticed through the big window a new young man was standing up in the dining room. Laurie recognized herself in him; he was standing like she was a few days ago when she was sending light to the stain glass sticker. From her chair, she could see the smile on his face despite his facial bruises, sores, and stitches. He gazed around the room, excited, looking for someone to talk to. She joined him, mostly out of curiosity. He noticed Laurie approaching and immediately seemed at ease with her. They introduced themselves and then Laurie asked,

"What happened to your face Jeff?"

"I had a car accident." Jeff seemed to be embarrassed and proud at the same time. Jeff smiled and added, "I decided to speed up and drive into a pole to prove to my mother that I am God!"

"And now, does she believe you?" Laurie asked without judgment.

"I don't think so, that's why she brought me here!"

"Well, I believe you. What are you going to do now?"

Jeff started looking away toward the heavens. He seemed relieved and said,

"I'm going to prove to the world that I'm back."

Laurie smiled at him again hoping he was right.

"It's good that you are here."

But Jeff simply nodded his head, and he was back in his thoughts as he remained quiet.

Laurie looked around and saw Dominic looking at them. He was alone sitting at his usual place with a chess game in front of him. Laurie joined and asked if she could play with him.

"Uh, well, do you know how to play?" he asked, seeming interested to play with her.

"I've played before," Laurie replied excited.

Within her unusual excitement, without boundaries between worlds and possibilities, Laurie wondered if Dominic could be the older brother she would have had if her mother's first child had not sadly been a miscarriage.

As soon as Dominic began to explain the rules, Laurie experienced a weird phenomenon. It seemed like another soul was in her etheric body; another little girl was with her. As she was back in her childhood, with a smile on her face, sitting on her knees, elbows on the table, her eyes fixed on the game, Laurie was extremely attentive to the instructions. She was aware some of her behavior was weird. But Dominic seemed amused as if he had found his little sister. There were no more barriers between them.

After the first game, he told Laurie he was impressed, and he didn't think she knew how to play! He encouraged her, "I really think you did good moves." Proud and happy to remember that sense of pride that comes when you are encouraged by your big brother, Laurie asked if they could play another game soon. "I'm up for it whenever you want," Dominic told Laurie with a warm smile which Laurie smiled back proudly, realizing Dominic had let his guard down with her. In the invisible, the little girl sharing her etheric body jumped at him and hugged him hard. Dominic didn't seem to notice anything. Laurie questioned if it was a part of her or another soul trying to be in contact with him. Because she didn't like the idea of sharing her etheric body, Laurie decided to believe he was her second big brother in a different parallel! Strangely, once Laurie was far enough away from Dominic, the little girl disappeared and Laurie regained full control of her thoughts and actions, no longer feeling duplication or interference around her.

Later after dinner, as Laurie was leaving the dining room, Brandon arrived with Isabelle and Nicolas. Right at the end of the corridor, they hugged, cried, and they laughed. They began chatting with the other patients. Mr. Mathieu told Laurie how lucky she was to have so many visitors. Laurie was proud but became uncomfortable noticing her friends were making too much noise, so she encouraged them to follow her in the dining room. She introduced them to Alexandre, Dominic, Sébastien, and Mr. Wilfred. But again, Laurie became uncomfortable noticing the patients' discomfort, so she asked her visitors to go to her room. Her friends were careful not to talk about the stunt during the student protest, thinking it was the reason for her hospitalization.

When the visit had come to an end, Isabelle and Nicolas hugged their friend letting her know she was important to them. Before reaching the two other friends, Brandon also hugged Laurie with love, closely sharing his thoughts in her ears, "It's been a good night tonight! Don't you think?" He was right. Laurie only had realistic talks, no visions, or phenomenon while walking in the corridor with them... but she sensed Brandon was thinking her normal behavior of tonight might be related to the increase of her medication. She remembered he wanted her medication to be increased. Laurie decided not to share with him that she knew about the higher dose of medication prescribed to her.

Brandon added,

"I spoke with your brother. Most likely he will come see you tomorrow night."

"What did he say?" Laurie asked surprised.

"Not much. He didn't know that you were at the hospital. He just told me he'll come to see you tomorrow. I also spoke to your father yesterday. I think Peter told him a bit about what happened to you. He said he'll try to come by and see you at the end of the week."

It was the first time Laurie thought about her dad and her brother.

Concerned about what they could think of her being hospitalized on floor six, Laurie tried to hold her tears. Brandon noticed his girlfriend's pain. He hugged her again very tightly. "Don't worry about that Lo. It can happen to anyone." Laurie was unable to utter a word, Brandon went on, "I'll stop by tomorrow if your brother can't come. Otherwise, I'll see you on Monday."

Laurie nodded her head letting him know that she understood. She then watched him through the window of the big blue door as he left. Seeing his girlfriend sad, he waved goodbye and blew her a kiss until she was out of sight.

Laurie was still feeling a little sad while walking to sit with the other patients for a snack before bed. But to see Mrs. Esther smiling while walking down the hallway with Sophie the nurse made her feel better. Curious to see them walking hand in hand, as she sat, Laurie asked the other patients if they had ever seen Mrs. Esther smiling and being kind like that. Mr. Mathieu, who was the only person who knew her well enough answered, "Besides Alexandre, she is always mean with people. I've never seen her smile before."

When they returned from their walk, Mrs. Esther exuded joy. The old lady came close to Laurie, waved, and smiled happily at her. Laurie felt proud thinking perhaps the visions they shared last night might have freed Mrs. Esther from her internal prison.

As she looked at Mrs. Esther leaving and entering her room, next door, another lady exited. Laurie had never seen her before, and she was fascinated by the way the lady exited the room, coming out as if she was a scientist departing a laboratory after many years of research. Of course, by the way she was dressed, everything helped corroborate Laurie's thoughts. She was dressed in a blue hospital robe, she had medium length, salt and pepper, tangled and spiky hair. Laurie thought she had just blown something up, like she had followed an experiment with test tubes and liquid. Laurie was amused to see the lady looking surprised with her hair all tangled up—she seemed like a mad scientist who had just experienced a major breakthrough. According to her joyful demeanor, most likely the experience was successful.

The lady was looking in all directions, searching for someone to talk to. While Laurie was entertained to see the peculiar character of the lady and her gesture, she had a vision of a beautiful reddish-brown rooster standing at her feet. The rooster was walking in her footsteps, making funny movements with his neck while looking in all directions as she did. At the same time, because this lady seemed like she was back from afar, and because of her thin frame body like her mom had, Laurie contemplated for a second it could be her mother returning from another world. But she put that thought aside, reasoning it was impossible.

Finally, the lady approached the group, seeming to be looking for controversy with her strange questions asked in such a provocative tone. Most of the patients were trying to escape her gaze, while Laurie smiled trying to find the part of her that reminded her of her mother.

"What are you smiling about?" The lady asked Laurie offensively

"Sorry. You remind me of my mother."

She turned away quickly as Laurie remained calm but laughed internally when she once again saw the rooster following her steps. Calmer, the lady then turned back and looked at Laurie, smiling this time as she was willing to talk.

"What do I have that makes you think of your mother?"

Spontaneously, Laurie responded,

"Your tiny body, your smile, and your confidence. Do you want to walk a little? You seem to have a surplus of energy!" Laurie asked as she stood in front of her, satisfied to detect the lady had just lowered her guard with her. Confirming Laurie was right, the lady smiled,

"Yes, you're right. I need to move!"

Seasol joined them and they walked two lengths of the corridor, laughing about discussions mostly based on craziness. Julie wasn't a biologist as Laurie and Seasol thought. Just before entering her room for the night, she admitted she was a teacher by profession.

As Laurie passed in front of the nurse counter to go to her room, a nurse gave her medication.

"I'll take it with water in my room," Laurie said as she continued on her way.

Thinking about her day and the great moment spent with her friends, Laurie peacefully fell asleep until the morning.

~ 20 ~

What do you Have? You don't Look Sick!

It was Mother's Day. Laurie called her best friend Arianne who recently was a mother of two amazing young kids. "Happy Mother's Day Ari," Laurie said holding her tears because of the shame she felt of being at the hospital. Brandon had informed Arianne a little bit about what was happening to Laurie but pretended to not know anything. Arianne was just extremely relieved to hear from her friend. Laurie explained to her briefly that she had entered the hospital because of weird phenomena that had happened to her.

With a comforting voice filled with love, Arianne said, "It's going to be okay Laurie. There's nothing there. It can happen to anyone. My mom and I are going to pray for you. I love you, and I'll see you soon."

Crying, but grateful that her friend was still thinking of her despite everything she probably had heard, Laurie quickly ended the call. When she walked out of the small cabin-like area, with red and puffy eyes, she saw Brandon at the counter, waiting for a nurse to give him back a copy of his novel.

"Why did you give her your novel?" she asked surprised.

Brandon answered calmly, "They said you had talked about my book, and they wanted proof that it was true. Who were you talking to on the phone?"

"To Arianne."

Laurie's happiness resurfaced as she thought of her and her children.

Brandon and Laurie decided to spend the time in the room and took the opportunity to exchange news, especially updates from the publishing house. Everything seemed normal. Before dinner, Brandon gave her a big hug and then he was on his way.

Laurie went back to the big room and sat next to Alexandre. In front of the TV, they were chatting about their time in high school and the friends that each other had and with who they were still in contact with. When Alexandre talked about one of his longtime friends, Maxime, and described where he was and what he was doing, Laurie immediately felt like she was transported on one of the boats, on the vast sea. Astonished, she saw on the dock, militaries dressed in white uniforms. In a rapid and special way, Laurie felt their emotions of adrenaline, pain, courage, sadness, hope, relief and pride passing through her. Interested by the Canadian Navy, Laurie asked him many questions and Alexandre was proud and eager to talk about his friend's career. And for a long time, they continued talking of each other's traveling adventures around the world.

After dinner, Laurie was lying on her bed. While trying to meditate, she began to feel a strong energy turning red, seeming to spray love, coming from the elevator. Despite the improbability of her three-year-old god-daughter being authorized to visit her, Laurie thought it could be her anyway. One minute later, her brother Patrick arrived with his daughter Mathilde. Amazingly, Laurie had felt her niece's presence coming filled with love. She shared this phenomenon with her brother as she hugged him, then she hugged and kissed her niece strongly like she liked to be kissed and tickled. Laurie gave them a tour, showed them the little dragon made of a piece of wood that she had painted during the afternoon activity, and took news from him before they had to leave.

Laurie went back to sit down with the patients for the evening snack.

"Is the little girl your daughter?" Julie asked as if all the other patients wanted to know also.

"No, she's my goddaughter, and he's my brother."

"I thought she was your daughter since she looks just like you," Mrs. Rita said slowly.

Laurie was beyond satisfied with that comment. She added proudly,

"Yes, we get that a lot."

Even though Laurie profusely blushed at the abundance of attention, Julie asked another question,

"What are you doing here? You don't seem sick! You're smiling, you help people, you are walking confidently, you have a lot of visitors! What do you have?"

Laurie was surprised and became rather shy at this moment since Mrs. Rita, Sébastien, and the three men: Mr. Mathieu, Mr. Wilfred and Félix were still listening. Seasol was also waiting for her answer. Laurie didn't know what to say but thank God, she had her book with her. A book she had never been able to read yet. Rather than giving an explanation, Laurie simply showed them the cover of her book. It was a picture of a young woman, smiling, dressed in a long red dress and dancing in a wheat field. Although Laurie had no idea what the story was about, she passed the book to them so they could read for themselves the title; *She Dances with Madness*. Julie seemed skeptical and Laurie had the feeling she considered her to be an impostor. Fortunately, the other patients seemed not bothered with the reason for her hospitalization.

Laurie quickly withdrew to avoid further questions. Lying on her bed, she prayed this time for her brother and his family, for Arianne and her family, for Brandon, and for all her other close ones. Without being able to finish naming them all, Laurie fell asleep peacefully until she awoke the next morning.

Eventually, Laurie was allowed to wear her clothes. Even if her pair of jeans and her white t-shirt were apparently a bit too big now, Laurie walked proudly meeting the other patients for the afternoon activities either outside, or inside cooking, painting, yoga...

While waiting for the next step, which would be to spend a weekend at home to see how it goes, Laurie was working on her concentration. To change her mind, sometimes she colored mandalas and shared her crayons with her friends who seemed to enjoy the benefit of it. One time, even Pascal had come and colored with her a few lines while looking so happy. She spent time with Sébastien who showed her his poems and drawings. She was playing chess with Dominic who was becoming a good friend. Even Brandon one night had played chess against him, and Laurie appreciated the mood. There were many times Laurie played nurse to Mrs. Rita by putting a wet rag on her arms to help diminish the swelling. With Seasol, who seemed to only need a good friend, they listened to other patients sharing about their pain.

She helped Mr. Wilfred, Félix, and Mrs. Madeleine during the afternoon activity at the gym, so they could benefit from exercising while the nurse was busy with either other patients or on her cellphone. That day, Kali, the nurse in charge of the daily activities asked Laurie to stop helping the others, saying they must learn to ask. Thinking it was ridiculous, luckily Laurie kept it to herself. She had all these bad resentments coming back, thinking of authority, power, the need to control by leaving the others in ignorance. Laurie looked at nurse Kali without understanding. *Why is she telling me that?* She was about to judge her; by the way she was always well-groomed, well dressed and wearing her high-heeled shoes. *In a hospital. Frankly!* Wisely, Laurie explained to the nurse she was just showing them how the exercise machines work, so they can enjoy their moment.

"I understand you want to help people, and you do it very well! But we want you to think about yourself first."

Laurie appreciated her words.

"Thank you for being concerned about me. I appreciate it but be reassured that I listen to myself first. If I help someone, it's because I can. That's because someone has already given me the advice, and I appreciate it when I can give back to others."

Kali left and Laurie felt proud to have made her point heard.

***

Friday morning, Laurie met Dr. Dion in her room.

"I heard that you were participating in every activity, and you are helping others."

Laurie smiled, waiting for her to continue.

"Do you feel ready for a weekend outside?"

"Of course." Laurie said surprised.

Seeming happy, Dr. Dion continued saying, "I will speak with your boyfriend and allow you a temporary leave for Saturday afternoon until

Sunday before dinner. We are encouraged to see how it goes for you on the outside."

Brandon had come to see his girlfriend almost every day and he was still there for her. He was waiting for Laurie, whose eyes filled with tears when she saw him, waiting for her at the nurses' counter with a rose in his hand. Outside, they were walking hand in hand to the car, and very gallant, he opened the door of his van for her.

"Thank you for picking me up." she said moved.

On their way home, Laurie expressed her needs by saying that she doesn't want to see anyone, that she doesn't know what happened to her, that she still feels fragile, and she wants to make sure she is okay before seeing her friends. Brandon understood and told her jokes to make her laugh and change her mind.

When they arrived in front of the apartment block, and when Laurie looked at the middle floor, she blushed immediately remembering what she had told her uncle the day before she was hospitalized. *The door of evil!* Laurie wanted to forget this event. She greeted her downstairs neighbors who were sitting on their terrace, gazing at her, seeming to wonder where she had been all this time.

Laurie had trouble breathing when she climbed up the stairs. The apartment smelled musty, the curtains were half closed and the floor was dirty. She went to her room to drop off her belongings and held back tears so as not to cry when she saw the pile of laundry, the papers hanging all over her desk and her bed half made. That mess reminded her of the state of mind she was in before she left the place last time. She took a deep breath and encouraged herself before starting to clean the place with difficulty. On his part, Brandon was smiling. He had not noticed the obvious disorder. For him, the only thing he noticed and disliked would be dirty dishes on the counter. Laurie didn't make any derogatory comments—after all, he had done so much for her lately and that was much more important! They ordered food and ate in front of the television. During the two shows that they watched, nothing out of the ordinary happened to her.

Once in bed, Laurie appreciated Brandon's presence with his warm body next to her. She felt excited and touched his foot with hers to see if he would react. Brandon immediately reacted. With his strong kisses, he proved to her that no matter what had happened, he still loved her. In return, she gave him her body and all her tender appreciation. Their bodies were exhausted. Laurie put her right hand on his strong torso, and he put his hand on her hair and caressed her as he wanted to help her fall asleep peacefully.

The next day, Brandon drove Laurie back to the hospital. She was happy knowing she was going to see her new friends. She felt that she was truly helping them, and in a way, she felt valued. In addition, the food was delicious and nourishing, and she didn't have to do household tasks.

At the end of the corridor, waiting for dinner, everyone kindly greeted Laurie. The men were talking and laughing together. Dominic and Sébastien took an extra moment and smiled at Laurie, seeming happy to see her back. Madeleine and Diana were talking together. Laurie had got to know them during the afternoon activities. Seasol had just sat next to Laurie and Julie was waiting on her own, standing outside her room, looking much calmer. Mrs. Esther was in her room, smiling while looking at the people passing in the corridor.

Satisfied to see her friends feeling better, that night, Laurie fell asleep wishing she would be with Brandon.

***

Tuesday, May 29th, eleven a.m. Two weeks from the first time Laurie had entered that room. She knew Dr. Dion might give her leave of absence today, but she felt nervous because she had not been totally honest with her. Waiting for her meeting with her doctor, Laurie straightened the blue cover on each side of her bed to have it clean. Impatient, she gazed at the city of Aliville through the big window and wondered if she should confess her secret—she was anxious the doctor wouldn't allow her hospital discharge. Laurie realized how much she would love to enjoy the summer outside, to enjoy being with Brandon, to see her friends, drive her car... she wanted to get her life and freedom back.

Knowing she was about to bring good news, Dr. Dion entered the room, happily greeted her patient, and sat on the visitor's chair. She asked her patient what her weekend was like.

"Well, I was surprised when I arrived home. Because I had to do some washing and cleaning, and many other chores to tidy up."

Understanding, Dr. Dion smiled lightly and asked how she had found her hospital stay so far.

"I think it's been good. It felt very good to be able to rest and not to have to prepare meals. I really liked the nurses because they listened to me, and I was able to free myself. But now I'm ready to go home. To get my life back! What do you think?"

Seeming happy, Dr. Dion told Laurie she seemed ready to go home. Surprised to be receiving so easily the green light to leave, anxious, Laurie asked her doctor,

"What do you think happened to me?"

"It's hard to say. You are in your thirties, and this is the first time you have been seen here with a mental disorder. We wrote in your file that it could have been a Transient Psychosis."

"How can you be sure that I'm ready to leave?"

"Because you are not like the first time I saw you. You're calmer, your eyes are more present! What you are saying is more rational. You sleep well, you cooperate well. You participate in the activities offered and you also help. Your reactions are good."

As she noticed the worried look on her patient's face, Dr. Dion asked, "Laurie, are you worried of leaving?"

Laurie looked down and took a deep breath. Her heart was beating fast. She was undecided whether she should confess or not. Laurie finally looked straight at Dr. Dion.

"I'm a little concerned. Like you say, I also think I'm doing better. But I must tell you... do you remember the day you wanted to increase my medication and I wasn't okay with that?"

Dr. Dion nodded unsured. Laurie continued, "We were supposed to keep the same dosage! Do you remember?"

"Yes." Dr. Dion said with a frown.

"When I put the pill on my tongue that evening, I sensed that pill was heavier than usual, so I took it off immediately and put it on a Kleenex. I didn't want to swallow it."

Dr. Dion was attentively listening.

"I know you increased my medication because during that night, a nurse entered my room with a flashlight, and noticed that I wasn't asleep. She told me my medication had been increased. So, I completely stopped taking the medication that same day."

Confused, Dr. Dion was silent. Laurie continued,

"I'm sorry that I took that long to tell you, but I wanted you to know before I leave."

Laurie waited for a response, but the doctor remained silent, seemingly trying to understand... *How could this be possible? The nurses are supposed to give her medication every night! And how many days are we talking about? It's been about ten days that Laurie had a higher dose of medication prescribed but didn't take it! How could she seem okay? How could she sleep all those nights? Is she playing with me? But if she's telling the truth, what is her new diagnosis?*

Laurie was eager to hear her doctor's thoughts.

"So, what do you think?"

Trying to hide her concern, Dr. Dion finally looked at Laurie and she responded,

"Thanks for sharing this information with me. There's not much we can do. Only time will tell. But for now, what do you think is best for you? Stay or leave?"

"I prefer to leave, and as you say, time will tell!"

Dr. Dion approved Laurie's discharge because for now she seemed okay. She prescribed her an antimanic drug in case she needed it and provided her direct phone number so Laurie could reach her if needed.

To be reassured, Laurie asked her doctor if they could meet again later and talk about it. "Of course," the doctor said and gave her an appointment in two weeks from now—Monday, June 11th at eleven am.

Rather satisfied with their discussion, Dr. Dion got up and said she will call Brandon to confirm that he can pick her up in the afternoon.

"Good luck, Laurie," Dr. Dion said sincerely before leaving. Emotional, Laurie stood up and thanked her doctor.

~ 21 ~

Back at Home

Laurie was back at home. All the windows were wide open, and the air was soothing to breathe. The heat and the sun's rays coming inside the apartment embellished her and made her feel like she was where she needed to be. Yet, standing in her kitchen contemplating the room, she felt uneasy thinking that she might not have fully healed. *Honestly, how could I be cured? And how could I be back to "normal" after having so many supernatural experiences? Would I have my body used again as a traveling tool for energy? Could I still have visions be so intense that they would prevent me from sleeping for several days? Could I be hospitalized again?*

In the uncertainty of the situation, with an extended break from work until her next doctor's appointment, Laurie planned to relax, to inform her loved ones that she's back home, but wasn't ready to see them yet. She wanted to put aside her last few weeks and talk about it as little as possible.

To be on the safe side, Brandon suggested to Laurie to have a friend sleep over, or to go sleep at her brother's house on the nights he had to go to work. Laurie appreciated his attention but declined his suggestion. Even though she felt a little fear knowing she would be alone, she told him that everything would be fine. "And Dr. Dion prescribed me pills in case I feel the need. Also, I can call you if I wake up at night and can't get back to sleep." Brandon had agreed. In the mornings, every time he came back from work, he asked his girlfriend if something special or unusual had happened during the night. The answers were always negative until the second Thursday...

The morning came slowly, and Laurie hadn't slept since her partner left the apartment around 1 am to go to work. All night she was wondering if she should take the pill or call her boyfriend but concluded no pill since nothing special was happening and a little insomnia didn't deserve worrying Brandon. *I'll find sleep with Brandon in the morning!*

When Brandon arrived, Laurie was waiting for him in the doorway. She asked him how his night was.

"Not bad. What about yours?" he said while kissing her.

"I didn't really sleep since you left but I'll go back to sleep with you now," she answered, thinking she was fine.

Lying on her side, Laurie's eyes were fixed on Brandon who was sleeping on his back. She gazed at his closed eyes and at his entire human body; his arms were down along his belly; his pale skin full of freckles and his torso was covered with red hair. She began to caress his right arm as well as his hairy torso. She slowly passed her fingers through his hairy chest. Brandon began to snore. Laurie looked up at his face, then looked at his lips, his chin, and his neck. Strangely, like a hologram, the presence of a feline body appeared and covered the majority of his body!

Brandon began to snore louder as his entire body was covered by scintillating and splendid fur, like a striped black and orange tiger. Laurie wasn't afraid and caressed him again, but this time with different touches. He was so soft and so majestic that every precious touch was in harmony with her breathing. She had no rational thoughts, and the memories of her last weeks were far behind. Laurie simply accepted what she was seeing and appreciated deeply the idea of lying next to a magnificent tiger belonging to another dimension. She venerated the idea that her boyfriend could take the shape of a huge wild cat. She felt so small beside him but with a wonderful reassuring and comforting feeling. Tears of joy, or fatigue, flowed down her cheek as she listened to him purr, sometimes roaring, making incredible decibels that the whole block could hear through the open window of the bedroom.

Unlike the usual nudging to help him stop the annoying snoring, this time she was looking at him with intense love. She was aware that she was living a special moment, and she welcomed this moment with a lot of love and respect. Madness? No. This idea never even crossed her mind, even though her reality and her imagination blended into each other. While admiring the two bodies, Laurie wondered if it was her way of seeing that had changed, or was it Brandon's body that was transforming? Because strangely, like a 3D image, when she was looking at Brandon's eyes, visibly his human body appeared; surrounded by materials such as the bed, the walls, the wardrobe behind... and when she shifted her gaze to his chin, his feline body reappeared like being in another dimension, another era, and another environment... *Unbelievable!* Laurie was in deep admiration with this phenomenon since Brandon's Chinese sign was the tiger! To confirm it again, she looked at his tattoo on his left pectora and it was indeed a tattoo of a roaring tiger like she remembered.

She caressed her half-man half-animal boyfriend with a new sensation, a new excitement never known before. The hologram showed an image of the feline with all his four legs pointing to the sky with his wrists hanging loose. He seemed to express his well-being, strength and beauty and nothing would prevent him from prolonging his nap. Laurie desired him with all her being. Strange impulses, seeming to come from the depths of her, manifested and ran through her whole body, which made her feel like a powerful tigress... Her caresses became more and more fierce as he roared louder and louder. When she moved up to look at her loved one straight in the eye in order to let him know that she would do anything to seduce him, a pleasant idea of her being a goddess before began to shimmer in her thoughts. A quick vision of a goddess in the heaven garden next to a guardian tiger appeared, but unfortunately, this image was brief as Brandon pushed her gently but firmly, encouraging her to rest a little more.

Still lying on the bed with her eyes sparkling and a smile on her lips, Laurie stared at the ceiling without feeling irritated. Brandon snored louder as direct rays entered the room. She let herself be lulled, intoxicated by these new images that paraded before her. The image of her father-in-law appeared slowly in front of her, as if he was floating in the air. As Laurie had always known, he was tall and strong, but he often looked upset or offended as if he always felt misunderstood by the entire world. Slowly, the image of him above was changing. He looked down, and looked intensely at Laurie, and then smiled affectionately. He seemed so different; he seemed to be happy!

When she wondered why her father-in-law was in her thoughts, the vision showed him becoming grandiose. He was sitting on a cloud and looking at her as if he wanted to make contact. He was wearing a simple white towel at the waist. Laurie was surprised to see him with a massive muscular torso, and even more stunned to see his hair and beard rejuvenated, growing long so quickly, and turning black and shiny. His smile, which she thought was often forced, was now radiant and full of happiness. Without judgment and as if by magic, the idea that he was Zeus, the God mentioned in legends, manifested itself in her thoughts. *Is that possible?*

Is that possible? She wondered again, hoping it was, because it was so wonderful. As she accepted this possibility, instantly a reaction between them both took place. The father-in-law, or Zeus, and Laurie laughed together. Even though they seemed to be in two different dimensions, the vision seemed palpable. As she appreciated this phenomenon, with a spontaneous gesture, the father-in-law moved his head backwards and let out a hollow, loud, and sincere laugh. He pointed down at his daughter-in-law with his index finger and with a proud look, he began to contemplate around him on his higher level. Slowly Laurie began to see what he was seeing; other gods were with him and what Laurie understood was that they allowed her to see them! They were all smiling, and the interaction seemed friendly. All were willing to say *he had won the bet!* The other gods designated him as the winner of this bet; he was the first perhaps for a long time, to have created an interaction between gods and humans.

Laurie was still lying beside Brandon. Incredulous with tears flowing without restraint, she wanted to believe this story of gods. But at the same times she was confused. It was a lot to accept, understand and rationalize since she had never really heard about gods besides in comics or fiction movies. Fortunately, the *Eternals* understood her questionings and immediately, with tenderness, they reassured her by whispering that it was indeed the reality; "We have existed since its inception. We are truly alive."

In a gentle and amused way of saying, a goddess added; *"And the reason why Zeus is so happy right now is that this time, it's a mortal of his lineage who discovered us!"* Laurie was speechless; a goddess had just confirmed what she was previously uncertain about.

With a sense of pride in this idea of sharing a moment with them, the vision of these gods that were among a few puffy clouds in a huge blue sky, quietly faded away. Despite their disappearance, Laurie felt an incredible understanding of their complexity growing in her. *But how did humans come to forget these Immortals?* And immediately, a memory of power-hungry people presented itself again as a vision. Some men of power had come to burn the scrolls or ancient writings that might recall the existence of gods. Others had simply denigrated the existence of the Immortals by claiming to be nothing but fables. *And again, all this manipulation to keep power over people!*

Laurie was feeling a real contempt for this behavior. It was when she let out an irritated sigh that Brandon cleared his throat and asked her how she was doing. Laurie looked at him. He had his eyes closed and she was looking to see his feline body again, but it was gone! There was no longer any trace of it, nor of the gods. A little disappointed, she got up from bed, kissed him on the cheek and replied, "I'm fine, thank you. I'll see what I can eat. I'll let you sleep."

After a short nap, Brandon joined Laurie in the kitchen and simply told her, "Lo, I think you should call your doctor." Without arguing she responded he was right, and that she would call her doctor later that day. Satisfied with her answer, Brandon looked at her mockingly and seemed rather proud, "Did you try to rape me earlier?" With a seductive look, Laurie smiled at him remembering every little detail of her caresses but kept it to herself.

However, she wanted to know if her father-in-law also had experienced this moment, this vision about the gods and her. She asked Brandon to call his parents to catch up with them. She was mostly curious to know if his father would mention about their special experience. *Will he mention to*

Brandon about our meeting between the two worlds? Does he know that his soul is Zeus? With enthusiasm, while watching Brandon talking with his parents, she pleasantly thought, *Wow! His father is a god! Zeus other than that. Who would have thought?* But Brandon's father never mentioned their possible special experience, so Laurie pondered if she had simply imagined this morning's events.

A little disappointed that nothing had been said about the special phenomenon, Laurie dialed the phone number she had received from her doctor. Dr. Dion wasn't there today.

Dr. David answered, "I'm sorry Laurie, my day is full. But I see you have an appointment scheduled this coming Monday. Can you wait until then?" he asked, seeming out of options unless to lead her to the walk-in clinic if she can't wait.

Believing that everything always happens for the best, Laurie confirmed she could wait.

"Perfect. Do you have any ideas on what you can do to relax while waiting for your appointment?" Dr. David asked.

The simple words "to relax" instantly made her think of receiving a relaxing massage. She was already feeling the pleasant sensation of her tense body relaxing under these serene practices.

"Yes, I will try to have an appointment for a massage. I'm sure it will help me relax and sleep better tonight."

Dr. David told her it was a good idea and reminded her of her appointment on Monday at 11 am.

Strangely, instead of calling the lady she had in mind for a relaxing massage, she called Mr. Gilbert, a chiropractor she had met a few times. He answered with a welcoming voice and confirmed that he had an opening today at 2:30 p.m. Immediately, Laurie saw this as a sign that the gods were with her, and everything would be fine. "Great! Thank you and see you soon."

Thinking about the time she had before her appointment and visualizing the path she would take, Laurie realized it would be a good time to stop and see her good friend, Isabelle, at her cafe. She called her friend to make sure she would have time for a break. "Of course!" Isabelle said enthusiastically, "I always have time for you, my friend. Come on over."

Laurie finally left the phone and told Brandon she would meet her doctor on Monday, and today she would have a massage. Brandon wasn't too worried because he had met with a psychic the week before, to be prepared (in a way) for what was about to come for his girlfriend following her hospitalization. The psychic lady had reassured him by telling him after reading the cards he drew, "You don't have to worry anymore. Laurie will be just fine, you'll see. What is happening to her is only temporary. She needs this time to see what she has to see."

~ 22 ~

Other Beings are Among us

Isabelle and Laurie were emotional when they hugged tightly in the middle of the cafe among a few guests. Isabelle showed her friend a table where they could sit in order to be comfortable chatting.

The two friends were face to face. Isabelle had a view of the outside and Laurie had a view of the entire inside of the restaurant. Normally Isabelle talks a lot and uses a lot of expressions that always makes Laurie burst out laughing. But today, Isabelle listened. Laurie knew her friend had an open mind on mystical subjects. As if she had a gift for understanding people, Laurie felt her friend was once more reading the unspoken! Laurie was so relieved to talk to this friend during a time when she felt a huge need to express herself, release her thoughts on what she had understood lately about space-time–about the sorceresses. She freely let her friend know they had probably been friends in a past life and been called witches due to their sensibilities with the mystical. She also shared about the Chinese Zodiac signs, reminding her friend they were both Dragons. Isabelle listened, smiled, nodded affirmatively at her friend; confirming that she understood. But in fact, she was tightly holding Laurie's hands, trying to send her good vibrations while holding her tears of incomprehension towards Laurie's behavior.

Before leaving, Isabelle took Laurie's face in her hands, paused, and looked intensely at her with her blue eyes in tears.

Concerned, she said, "Take care of yourself, my friend. Call me anytime. I'll always be available for you. You know that right?"

She did not let go of Laurie's face until she believed in her friend's sincerity to have understood.

"I'm fine Isabelle. It's a weekday and I'm off. Plus, I'm going to get a massage. What more could I ask for?" Laurie said in a mocking way, smiling and grateful for her friendship. "Anyway, I'll see you tomorrow night at the girl's dinner?"

"You're right. It's at the new Irish pub! I can pick you up if you want?" Isabelle offered.

"I'd love to. I don't want to arrive alone for my first outing. It's weird but I can't wait to be at this new pub. It seems that the word 'Irish' inspires me, as if I've lived among them in another life!" Laurie told her again mockingly, giving her a wink, indicating that there was nothing to worry about with such an idea.

Laurie drove to receive her massage treatment and was thinking about her last visit with Mr. Gilbert. She had met the man about a year ago. He was in his 60s, he stood tall, strong, had a neat appearance with his thick white hair. Laurie had been pleased when she discovered that the pile of paper placed on the corner of his desk were prayers available to anyone interested.

She had been extremely satisfied with Mr. Gilbert's treatment for her shoulder, and even more satisfied with his philosophy of life when he had said, "Before I take care of someone, I always ask my Angel Guardian to guide me in order to offer the best of myself." With a mocking smile and pointing to the sky, he had added, "He knows more than me what has to be done."

During their few meetings, they had discussed astrology and cosmology. Feeling connected with this man, Laurie had told him that her mother had taken cosmology courses a very long time ago and she was discrete talking about it with other adults. Mr. Gilbert had shared with her that his wife and him had been affected a lot, when several years ago they had talked cosmology and the kind of beings in space, but some people were mean with them. They gradually stopped sharing what they were learning. To conclude, Laurie had shared with this open minded man that she had become interested in this science since the eve of her mother's passing, about three years ago.

Mr. Gilbert was dressed in a white uniform when he once again welcomed his patient professionally and warmly. Laurie was grateful that he had found time for her today. She liked the smell and warm atmosphere of the room. While he was practicing his maneuvers on her, she felt a great need to reveal to him a secret that she had kept to herself, also for fear of criticism from people. She told him her story about Mother Mary who had come to her and protected her from evil spirits that revolved around her when she was a teenager. She showed him how Mary had opened her arms horizontally and had pushed those entities away from her etheric body. "She freed me," Laurie said emotionally.

Following, Mr. Gilbert shared that he, too, had a wonderful moment with a supreme being. He had a vision and described the being as the guardian of the healing sword. "I think it was Orion. I saw him only once and only his upper body had appeared." The man was very proud about his experience but seemed to want more, as if he needed to see the being a second time to be certain of his beliefs. Although Laurie had a deep desire to tell him everything she had experienced in the last couple weeks, she resisted and simply told him that she sincerely believed him. During the last part of the treatment, Laurie prayed to the Lord and Mother Mary to give this great man the best of what he needs.

Once the treatment was over, for the first time, Mr. Gilbert accompanied his patient to the exit door since they had so much to talk about. He was still talking about mystic subjects when Laurie bent to put her shoes on. And suddenly, the man remained quiet in the middle of what he was saying. Laurie looked up at him. He had his eyes closed in a solemn position. She stood up quietly, delicately put her bag and keys on the chair to free her hands, stood back and took the same position as the man. She saw an energy appearing between them. Mr. Gilbert had his head leaning slightly backwards and he opened his arms along his body. He was in a trance and whispering sounds that she couldn't understand. But Laurie had the feeling this good man was experiencing a second contact with his guide of light.

Delighted, Laurie remained silent in order to let him live this moment which he seemed to have waited for so long. The energy lengthened, as if

He wanted to reveal its entirety. Laurie was captivated by the phenomenon. Her eyes had filled with tears, and she was grateful thinking her prayer had been answered once again. The arms of this kind man moved as if some energy was passing through him. Laurie breathed discreetly and deeply enjoyed what some would call a miracle.

After a long minute or so, Mr. Gilbert opened his eyes slowly seeming to enjoy every moment. In front of him, and having kept the same position, Laurie was calm, smiling and thrilled for him. Serene, he told her that this was the first time he saw his guide's full etheric body and thanked Laurie for staying and respecting this moment. Laurie confessed to him that she had also seen the white light. He looked at her and visibly shaken, he shared on his experience: his feelings, what he had thought during this phenomenon, what he had seen... Laurie listened to him and without a doubt, she believed everything he told her.

Laurie left the place thanking the universe for answering her prayer. She thought that this miracle was a reinforcement for Mr. Gilbert to keep believing in the way he treats and takes good care of his patients with an open mind and respect for the powerful energy above him. For a moment, Laurie thought she was the reason of this phenomenon because she felt she exuded so much energy since her experience as a lightning rod between two worlds. She thought Mr. Gilbert and his open mind had been in contact with his guardian angel through the light that surrounded her; in her etheric body. Yet uncertain, she put this thought aside while opening the door of her car. Grateful to have witnessed this miracle, she closed the door and stopped thinking about it, leaving this wonderful moment to be expressed by Mr. Gilbert if he wanted to.

***

That night, Laurie was unable to fall asleep. She tossed and turned and put the blame on her boyfriend's intense and noisy jerky breaths. Brandon finally left for work, which gave Laurie hope of being able to sleep. Two hours later, her bedside clock indicated three o'clock in the morning, and she was still wide awake.

She recalled her day when suddenly, like an out of body experience, her spirit was back when she was sitting with her friend Isabelle at her cafe. She was floating higher and from behind her physical body that was holding her precious friend's hand. She was seeing the entire inside of the café again as it was. Without paying too much attention, she saw again the man who had looked intensely in her direction throughout his walk to a banquet, yet further behind her friend. As a courtesy Laurie had smiled at him but he had maintained a cold look at her.

Why am I here? Laurie wondered and paid attention to her friend's eyes to verify if she had misinterpreted any of her signs during their chat. She saw Isabelle again exactly the same way, frowning, squeezing her hands when Laurie shared some revelations she had understood during her last weeks. Again, Laurie saw this man walking behind her friend, always staring at her before returning to his table. Like if Laurie was hypnotized, able to freeze the time, she observed the man. He was an average height, dressed in a blue shirt and beige pants. He had gray, curled and messy uncombed hair. He seemed to be in his fifties and behind his big square glasses, he always had a cold look.

Having noticed only a few new details of this man, Laurie brought her gaze back to her friend who had her blue eyes in tears, smiling affectionately before asking a question that Laurie could not understand in that special moment. The man walked again in the same direction and was staring again intensely at Laurie, as if he wanted her to understand something. Laurie began to be scared seeing this vision of this man walking always in the same direction and always staring coldly at her. *What does he want to tell me?*

Strangely, Laurie was realizing the man had walked in the same direction several times. In a unique way, each time, he was moving as if he stood on a conveyor rather than walking normally, and with his head moving only enough to keep his gaze always fixed on Laurie. Laurie didn't remember seeing him sit, as if, rather by magic, he became invisible and returned each time to his starting point so to pass and pass until Laurie saw him. *But I've seen you now!* Laurie said, anxious and tired. *What do you want?*

Terrified by the response she received, and what she thought she understood, her spirit immediately returned to her body. By reflex, she jumped in her bed. Afraid, she tried to hide under the blankets up to her chin. *He's an alien!* The intense unpleasant sensation that she might vomit was related to the understanding that this man was revealing his true nature. The air was hard to breathe. Laurie could feel his presence in her room. She felt suffocated as she was having trouble breathing. She wondered if she was currently in danger, and if he was a good or a bad Being. She wondered if this afternoon she had been the only one to see him. Courageously, Laurie tried to recall the face he showed her during the visions. His gaze was frigid, expressionless, and seemed strangely unfamiliar. Suddenly, she began to see the energy waves he had released each time towards her to create a contact as to say "Hello." And as if by telepathy, he helped her understand that vibrations were his way of communicating!

That's why it wasn't familiar to me! Laurie thought as she felt a little bit more informed. Somehow, this alien energy was asking Laurie to calm down and not be afraid. Quietly, a brown face appeared at the tip of her bed in the dark light of her room. The face had two large, glazed eyes as a mirror reflecting what he was seeing. Stunned, Laurie backed up quickly and waited for what would be next. Somehow, she knew he felt her emotions of fear and surprise. Gradually, coming at about a three-inch distance of her as if he was floating, he made her understand that he could take the form he wanted; human, alien, or also remain invisible if he wanted to. Laurie didn't feel so much fear for herself anymore. But the idea that he could walk among humans, without us knowing, frightened her. *And how many more are there? And what do they want?*

In the darkness of the night, Laurie could no longer see his face, but she still felt his presence. Bravely, she told him; *"If you have nothing more to say, go away. Now that I know what you may look like, I'll pay attention to those details."* Instantly, Laurie no longer felt his presence around her.

She no longer feared. She was rather incredibly surprised to have been in contact with an alien. *But why did he reveal himself to me?*

The possibility that Laurie may have hallucinated never entered her mind. While trying to make sense of an alien visit, Laurie remembered an event that happened when she was young, but she had chosen to forget. Her brother Patrick though, liked to tell this story of a small spaceship that had landed overnight on the street in front of their childhood house. He swore that the light had been so bright that most of the neighbors woke up overnight and went outside. He said he knew it wasn't a dream because his slippers were still wet in the morning. "The alien perhaps erased the memories of the people, but I remember, and you were with me, Laurie." Laurie was four-years-old, and she also believed it had happened. But slowly over the years, she was unsure if it had been true because her dad was telling her it wasn't true, and she was repeating her brother's stories. Patrick had told this story many times to whoever brought up the subject of aliens, but too many times people doubted. Because of the disbelief and judgmental looks on their faces (when her brother told this story with conviction) Laurie didn't want to talk about it anymore.

But tonight, for the first time since her childhood, Laurie truly believed this unbelievable event had happened in her childhood neighborhood. *We did meet with aliens before, just like I did tonight.* Laurie had no doubt she had met with one extraordinary being but wondered why he came so close to her.

The idea of trying to fall asleep was unthinkable. Laurie got up in the middle of the night and serenely walked throughout the dark apartment. She was looking at her many decorative hall masks. Impressed by their similarity to the alien, she tried them all on her face, waiting to feel any kind of vibrations. But nothing happened. Without emotion, she went back to her bed and tried to sleep... but couldn't.

~ 23 ~

The Aliens

Friday morning. The fatigue on Laurie's face was evident when her sweet boyfriend returned from work. Laurie went to bed with him, but Brandon had less patience than the day before. In the early signs that Laurie couldn't fall asleep, thinking it was because of the daylight, he suggested, "Why don't you put your mask on?"

Laurie stood up immediately, and rushed out while saying that it was a great idea. She walked quickly along the wall and searched for the perfect decorative mask. She picked the shiny black wooden mask with slanted eyes that came from Cuba, a souvenir from a vacation with her girlfriends many years ago. Satisfied with her choice, she went back to bed next to Brandon, and put the wooden mask on her face. Through the holes of the two narrow eyes, she looked directly at the ceiling, paying attention whether something special would happen this time, but still nothing. After a while of discomfort and restraint, she confessed simply, "It's not that comfortable! And I still can't sleep."

Half asleep, Brandon looked at her stunned, and burst out laughing, not believing what he was seeing. "Not this kind of mask! The one you put on sometimes to help you sleep and block the light." He stood up, uncertain what to think about this situation, went in to Laurie's drawer and got the one he had in mind, her soft sleepy mask.

Confused, as she returned to normal, Laurie laughed with him when she realized the nonsense of the situation. She thanked Brandon, put on the more comfortable mask, and tried to sleep like this event was only a misunderstanding. But after a moment, she gave up trying to fall asleep and oddly, decided to go and read.

She had few options of books but picked *Telos, Revelation of the New Lemuria*. It was a book belonging to Mr. Gilbert and he had lent it to her a couple of months ago. As she tried to continue reading it, she recalled it was about a community of different beings living inside the earth. The inner Earth inhabitants (as they were called) had extraordinary powers. Laurie wanted to know more about their story, but it was too difficult to concentrate so she called her brother; remembering he was off on Fridays.

It was decided. She would take advantage of her unusual day off and finally spend time with her brother this afternoon.

Brandon was sleeping in the guest room and Laurie was in her room with the phone still in her hand, looking at the patio door, thinking of how to get dressed. It was then that she saw a huge insect of about four inches walking on the floor towards her. Surprised, wondering what it was and where it came from, Laurie stepped back while deciding if she should step on it; despite its size, or if she should lock it up in the room and wait for Brandon to wake up.

The unusual insect stopped in front of Laurie, and she realized how beautiful it had become. It had the shape of a large ladybug and was covered with colorful reddish-yellowish fur. As Laurie was in admiration, this perfect creature turned back, returned moving like a spider with long synchronized steps, then managed to fit and disappear in an almost nonexistent hole between the floor and the base molding of the patio door.

Certain she wasn't hallucinating because she actually could have touched the creature, Laurie immediately assumed it could be an inner Earth inhabitant. *He had come to see me. Maybe I'm releasing so much energy lately that I might have fascinated the inner population?* Feeling so privileged to have witnessed this beautiful creature never seen before, Laurie wanted to make contact with this different being. Thinking it was using the same language as the alien of last night, Laurie sent him good vibrations trying to tell him, *come back, I want to meet with you!*

But sadly, the insect didn't come back. For a moment, she supposed it was a being who came as an explorer, and he was returning to his population reporting she wasn't ready to know more about them. The next moment, Laurie had in mind that it could be the alien from last night, who came back to show her his ability of changing the physical form to adapt in a different environment! As Laurie pondered that thought, she felt the energy of the weird man at the café, the alien in her room overnight, and the beautiful insect had the same energy vibrating. In this way of thinking, unusual creatures like dragons and fairies became as real as aliens. All those beings could become invisible or change from wonderful to scary beings depending on the situation they're in.

As she believed it, a vision appeared; in a kind of cave, a man was pointing his sword at a dragon in chains four times his size. Laurie thought the dragon would release flames to defend itself, but contrary of a counterattack, the dragon disappeared, leaving the man perplexed. *Wow, instead of fighting, the dragon simply became invisible. He still lives somewhere, perhaps peacefully in another dimension!* Laurie believed she had witnessed the supposed extinction of the dragon.

Laurie finally arrived at her brother's home. Patrick was working outside with pieces of wood. As he approached to greet her, Laurie saw the décor changing, and Patrick looked like a carpenter. Instead of the garage, it was an old wooden hut; instead of the asphalt, it was some kind of red dirt; instead of wearing a T-shirt, a pair of shorts and sneakers, Patrick was dressed in a long, beige tunic robe and ancient flip flops. The idea that her brother could have been Joseph, Jesus' dad was in her thoughts. Excited by this possibility, Laurie told the details of her vision to her brother; only mentioning he could have been a carpenter during a previous life... during Jesus's time.

Patrick laughed anyway as he hugged his little sister. They had a good time talking about Patrick's projects. Laurie encouraged him enormously as she believed everything was possible for him now.

Patrick began to sense his sister was more extroverted than usual. Awkwardly, he talked over her, saying he needed to go pick-up his daughter at kindergarten. Uncertain, he asked his sister, anyway, if she wanted to go with him, and Laurie accepted joyfully.

In the car, while looking at her brother driving, she sensed he somehow had a connection with aliens. Without filter, she said, "I don't know if it's because you believe in aliens, but it seems to me you could be one."

"Eh!" Patrick spontaneously let out, not believing what she had just said.

Laurie reminded him about the spaceship they saw when they were young. "Since then, you have always been interested to read and watch documentaries about aliens, as well as the Egyptians and their pyramids. Right?"

Patrick couldn't argue with that but found nothing to add.

When they arrived at their destination, Patrick was hoping Laurie would stay in the car, but she followed him in the backyard of the house. She was interested to see where her niece was spending all her time. While Patrick was talking with the home childcare provider, Laurie was feeling the place, looking at the little kids playing in a small fenced backward, under a big tree that gave a lot of shade. She was feeling the vibrations and it seemed to her that some kids were inhabitants from the inner earth. *The Lemurians!* She was delighted to finally meet them, and she was fascinated to notice none of them were playing together, as if each of them was in their own world. Her niece, Mathilde, wasn't talking much but was smiling with delight at her aunt. Laurie grabbed a ball and played with her. Then eventually, they were welcoming the other kids coming to play with them.

The kids didn't know how to catch the ball. Laurie spontaneously taught them so they could have more fun. Rapidly, the kids were playing together, laughing, and proud to finally be able to grab the ball and improve their dexterity. Because they learned so fast, Laurie thought they always knew how, but they were waiting for someone to show them, so they didn't overstep the human process. Mathilde was looking at her aunt. Seeming so proud of her aunt, like she wanted to say, *Thank you for accepting us as we are.*

Alerted by the new kids' laughs, the childcare provider noticed the kids playing cheerfully together with their new skills. Moved by what she was seeing, the lady told Patrick that his sister was pretty good with kids.

Patrick always knew his little sister had intuition. As they got into the car, he was grateful for this past moment. But unfortunately, this peaceful moment faded when Laurie said out of nowhere, "I think Mathilde's soul is connected with aliens from the inner earth."

Patrick added nothing until they got home. He went inside leaving the girls enjoying the outside. In her special way, Mathilde showed her aunt under which tree she likes to sit, and how she's good at taking care of insects, as if they were her friends.

Laurie was at peace while looking at her niece play with another kind of being. A little out of rationale, Laurie was amazed as she truly believed in a whole other world of intelligent beings living under the ground, changing their physical form to adapt and keep the anonymity when coming over to the earth. These ideas merged into Laurie's thoughts when Patrick called her. He approached her and gave her his phone. It was Brandon.

"Isabelle is waiting for you at home. Are you going to a girl's night tonight?" he asked, seemingly unhappy because of what he had just heard from Patrick about Laurie's strange conversations.

"Yes," Laurie said as she just remembered she had an evening planned. "Tell Isabelle to wait for me please. I'm coming right away."

She gave the phone back to her brother, hugged him, and then she bent and tenderly hugged her niece. Wishing to spend more time with them, she said before leaving, "It would be nice if you could come with us tonight."

While waiting for Laurie to arrive, Brandon shared with Isabelle that he didn't like the idea of her girlfriend going out in public, adding she might do or say stupid things, but Isabelle reassured him; telling him she would keep a close eye on her.

On her way home, thinking about the night to come with her longtime girlfriends, having no barrier of time and dimensions, Laurie had a strange sensation they had all been goddesses during a previous life. Like a blurry vision, she revisited the time when they were all together on vacation on the island of Cuba. They were all smiling, in peace, surrounded by the blue paradise of the ocean. It was like they were in a higher dimension, on top of a cloud, looking down on Earth, choosing to jump into nothingness and come to live a physical life. Like baby birds when they jump from their nest to go and learn more. Fiery, Laurie had the feeling tonight would be the reunion evening of their souls, their roots, where they truly come from, and what they did since.

She was thrilled about that thought and believed even more of this idea when she arrived home and saw Isabelle dressed all in white, sexy, and confident as she just came down from the goddess world. "Wow Isabelle, you look like a goddess tonight." Even Brandon seemed to agree while Isabelle was proud of this special compliment.

Isabelle and Laurie were the first of their group to arrive at this new Irish restaurant and bar. Laurie couldn't wait to see her other friends, but unfortunately, some of her friends were not in the same mood as her. Some friends had been told about Laurie's situation and they arrived a little anxious, unsure how to act with Laurie who was apparently experiencing a mental disorder. They had tried to postpone the girl's night, but Laurie had insisted.

Arianne arrived first and moved forward in an unusual neutral way, while looking discreetly at the place. Laurie barely recognized her friend since, like a 3D image, the décor changed for a vast and dry place; Arianne was entering a cave, and it was like she had used a temporal rift in space and time to come to this goddess reunion! She was dressed in a simple long brown piece of fur instead of a nice short white fur jacket. Her face and hair were dirty and messy instead of clean. She was holding a dead animal and a big wooden stick instead of her purse, and she was searching for her partner among the drunk Cro-Magnons instead of searching for her friends.

Laurie was jumping inwardly believing she was witnessing where her friend went and lived after jumping from heaven to come live a physical life. *She went straight to the prehistoric time!* Without filter, she tried to share her vision and thoughts, "Wow Ari, I had a vision, and it was like you had lived your first life on Earth during prehistoric times. You were a Cro-Magnon and had caught food to provide for your family. You succeeded in that life, and I think this is why you are so good in this one, at catching meat, preparing, and cooking food!" Beside blushing and smiling slightly, Arianne went to sit at the table trying to hide her tears.

Laurie hugged her friend Anne who followed behind. Anne was the friend who she had associated as a warrior fighting for her freedom in the movie of the battle between good and evil. She also seemed to have been using a temporal rift to come to this reunion. She seemed taller than usual. She had long glittering hair, was dressed in a leopard-patterned shirt, seeming to come from another previous life where she was defending the animal of the jungle. Always without filter, Laurie said, "I saw a movie the other day. I was sure it was a story about a previous life of yours. You were a warrior fighting for your freedom as I always considered you; a fighter!" Anne laughed slightly at this possibility and went to join Arianne.

Jennifer was following, dressed in a toga-style satin white shirt letting one naked arm reveal her new red roses tattoo. She looked glowing like she had just come down from her cozy cloud, instead of coming from an earthly life. "Wow Jen, you look like how a goddess could look." Flattered, Jennifer thanked her friend for her kind words and quickly went to sit with the others.

Elisabeth followed behind. She walked confidently even though she was oddly dressed in a brown vest and a pair of brown pants. Laurie had an image of her friend being Lancelot, one of the seven knights during the King Arthur historical time. Laurie hugged her friend trying to hold her emotions, realizing they had fought together for peace and freedom during the 5th or 6th century. Surprised by Laurie's strange behavior, Elisabeth kindly pushed Laurie away and quickly went to sit with the others.

Kevin (Anne's brother) had decided at the last minute to join the girls for dinner. They had not seen each other for a long time, and Laurie was happy to see him because due to his presence tonight, they were the same exact group of friends who were together during the vacation in Cuba! Laurie agreeably contemplated this moment with no doubt of the validity of her thoughts.

Grateful to be with her friend, Laurie sat at the end of the table and proclaimed to all, "Guess what, we are the same group that we were during our vacation in Cuba. And now, we are in an Irish pub. Isn't that wonderful?" No one added a word, and all returned to their conversation.

Strangely to Laurie, the Irish pub represented the place where King Arthur and the six knights had met after one of their fights. In a vague thought, Laurie believed they were the seven knights. She was reliving the time when they were back from war and were among the other citizens; finally feeling free. Excited, she wanted to celebrate and buy the first round of beer for her friends, but they refused. She wanted to discuss deeper ideas than usual, like passed lives, souls, where we come from, if they believed they lived during the King Arthur's epoch... but apparently, no one wanted to talk about those subjects. Laurie wanted to dance, but no one wanted to dance.

She went alone to the bar. In the dim light of the resto-bar, she saw an old, paralyzed man in a wheelchair and strangely, Laurie immediately thought he was her grandmother using the man's physical body to get in contact with her. The man had the same warm smile and sparkling eyes like her grandmother when he looked as Laurie approach him. With kindness, Laurie asked the man if he needed anything. Then she talked about the possibilities of one soul being able to use someone else's body. The man was smiling, happy for the attention. Rapidly Jennifer arrived and asked Laurie why she was talking to this man. "I'm talking with my grandmother." Laurie answered honestly.

Jennifer smirked holding her tears, then grabbed Laurie's hand guiding her, "Your friends want to see you at the table." Laurie followed and sat but only for a little bit because she became bored with the superficial subject they were talking about. Slyly, Laurie went back to talking with who she thought was her grandmother.

It was now clear for all that Laurie wasn't doing good. To protect her reputation, Arianne led the group and said, "I talked with Brandon. Laurie has a mental disorder, maybe because of the stunt they did during the manifestation, or it could be because of her mom passing four years ago. We are her friends, and we need to help her. She has an appointment with her doctor on Monday. We shouldn't talk about her behavior to anyone and if people ask what is going on with her, we should simply say that Laurie has a little depression. Let's go home, Laurie will follow." Everyone agreed.

Jennifer went back to get Laurie and kindly told the man to stop talking to Laurie even if she returns to him.

Everyone was about to leave when Laurie came back. All wished she would do the same, but Laurie didn't want to go home. She was feeling so alive in the Irish bar. "Without her consent, we cannot force her to leave," Arianne helplessly said to the other friends leaving with sadness.

Isabelle had decided to stay with Laurie; thinking she could help bring her dear friend back to reality. They sat together with a pitcher of beer on the table. Laurie was talking freely about her contact last night with an alien in her room, trying to make sense out of it and why it happened to her. In disbelief, Isabelle was listening not knowing what to say. Hoping Laurie would stop talking about unrealistic subjects, Isabelle waved at two acquaintances she knew that had just entered the bar, to sit with them.

Laurie was looking at Max, a famous man that probably the whole state of Quebec knew for his television show. She asked Isabelle how she knew him. "Max is from Aliville. You didn't know? The other guy is Michael, his good friend, and they are my cousin's friend." The men greeted many friends at the bar and then came and sat at Isabelle and Laurie's table.

Isabelle went to get two more glasses to share the pitcher of beer with them. While they were sitting and getting comfortable, Laurie was fascinated by Max. Not because of his popularity, but because she was realizing his true personality seemed to be just like the person he portrays on his show; always neutral, not expressing any emotions even when he should. *Exactly like the extraterrestrial from the café!* And oddly, his physical body resembled Laurie's brother, Patrick. And Michael, the other friend looked like, in a way because of his shy and nice smile, to her niece

Mathilde. Happy and confident, Laurie greeted them. She drew closer to the famous man and without filter she confessed, "You're an extra-terrestrial right?"

He smiled, amused by this new comment probably heard for the first time. He looked at Laurie, seeming interested and wanted to know more. Laurie continued, "I saw you many times in different shows, and it seems like you never express emotion. Right?" Max seemed to agree with her. "Aliens do not express emotions, but they communicate with vibration, right? I had a contact with one yesterday and I know how to detect you now," Laurie said joyfully, proud to have discovered their mystery.

Isabelle returned and requested to switch places after realizing what her friend was saying. She apologized to Max for the words of her friend and changed the subject. Once introduced to Michael, Laurie felt transported to another world. Again, without a filter, she began to share with him what she recently discovered about the inner earth inhabitants. Michael seemed to like the subject, so Laurie confessed to him that she was seeing him as someone coming from inner earth, like an elf with a pure heart, and surrounded by flamboyant colors; the opposite of the space alien who seemed more of cold and brown (without colors).

"I know people don't usually talk about these topics but what do you think? Don't you think that there are other beings living around us, inside the earth as well as in the space?" Michael smiled like he allowed his world to take life. He nodded timidly as he also believed in other lives.

Before leaving, the two men hugged Laurie telling her they had had a good time with her; adding it was rare but fun talking about topics like that. She was satisfied to have opened the discussion on a mystical subject. As she watched them leaving, curiously, they seemed very familiar, like it was in fact, her brother and her niece who came to spend time with her and put her to the test. *Because I told them to come, they came!* Laurie thought while being impressed on how advanced alien's and inner earth inhabitant's skills were to change physical forms.

Excited and thinking she had spent the last hour with her brother and niece, Laurie paid for another beer for her friend, wishing to talk more about taboo subjects. Hoping to get Laurie's rational thought back to normal, Isabelle confronted her. Unfortunately, this wonderful night ended with Isabelle and Laurie's first feud ever. They left the bar; each one went on their way. Remembering the promise made to Brandon, Isabelle tried to get Laurie in the car, but Laurie firmly declined the offer. She didn't like to be called "crazy."

"Isabelle, you are too frustrated with me. Let's calm down and let's talk later." While Laurie continued walking towards home, Isabelle called Brandon who came right away to pick up his girlfriend. But Laurie was almost home and preferred to continue walking, clearing her mind, and finding the right way of talking about mystical subjects.

In the middle of the night, shocked and unannounced, Isabelle went to see her parents who knew Laurie well. Uncontrollable, Isabelle screamed, and cried for many hours trying to let go of all her anger and stress towards Laurie.

~ 24 ~

Lost in Other Realities

In the morning, Laurie had tried to convince Brandon that the argument with Isabelle the night before was nothing to worry about and they were still friends. Anyway, Brandon needed to leave, supposedly he had work to do for the publishing house.

Alone, lying on the couch, Laurie wasn't feeling well at all, and she prayed for help. Fortunately, Aunt Angela called and invited her to have lunch with her and Uncle Peter. Laurie gratefully accepted the invitation and spent the afternoon and had dinner with them as well. Still, Laurie didn't have filters and shared her thoughts as freely as they came. Yet, with them, she wasn't thinking about aliens. Instead, from time to time, her new reality was taking place in the story of Asterix and Obelix; a comic strip based on the idea of powerful and invincible villagers (The Gauls), defending their village and their freedom against Rome.

Confused in-between realities, in the back of her head, it seemed to Laurie that her town Aliville was that village, and her relatives and friends were represented by the characters from the comic strip. She spoke freely relating Uncle Peter with Obelix, Aunt Agela to the wife of the leader of the group, and her dad to be Asterix.

Throughout the day, Laurie went from one subject to another, talking about the visions she was seeing. It seemed she was traveling through many other realities. She saw Uncle Peter surrounded by plants with big shiny green leaves and a colorful parrot beside him. The entire vision seemed to suggest that Peter was the chief of a tribe, he was in a parallel world, somewhere in the jungle in South America. Although astonished by Laurie's imagination, Peter could see some sort of similarity between those worlds. Sometimes he would laugh, sometimes he would say she exaggerated, but most of the time, he thought Laurie's behavior was because she had consumed too much drugs.

It was dark when they finished dinner. Aunt Angela and Uncle Peter had found the right words to tell Laurie she wasn't thinking rationally again. Sad, Laurie agreed. But she didn't know what was happening to her, all she was doing was coping the best she could in the present moment. She looked out of the window and at the sight of the church on the mountain, she felt inspired. She thought by going to the Sunday morning mass, she would be healed. "I will stop by the church on my way home to find out what time mass is tomorrow," she simply said, thinking it could reassure them.

Once Laurie was gone, Angela called Brandon to let him know Laurie, again, shared a strange discussion but was now on her way home. Angela was worried and asked Brandon to give her news as soon as he could.

*****

It was pouring when Laurie arrived at the church parking lot. As Laurie was looking to find the mass hours, many other cars were arriving behind her. Laurie felt destabilized since she hadn't expected a special event to happen on a Saturday night. People were running to get inside the church. For a moment, Laurie thought they had come to help her and to pray for her. It was as if each of them had been called by a higher being. Although grateful, she wondered about her clothing and her hairstyle that were clearly inappropriate for the occasion. But in despair, she simply asked for forgiveness to God, then entered the church and joined a crowd who didn't really pay attention to her.

The ceremony had not started yet. Many people were waiting in line to shake hands with the priest, other were seated, chatting, and laughing together. It was different to all her other visits. Confident, Laurie walked along the aisles, and looked carefully at the stained glass on each window on the first floor. Throughout those images of the stained glass, she was revisiting the history of Jesus. She slowly became euphoric, feeling a huge part of the universe was explained in that church.

She headed towards the second floor, and while she walked up the stairs, she had the impression she was crossing to a higher dimension. She

188

pleasantly thought her intuition was right as she realized the stained glass on the second floor was representing the astrological signs. She understood that around and far above Jesus' physical realm, and humankind, there was a superior dimension, with the wholeness of the astrological sign protecting the earth.

Laurie solemnly stopped in front of each of the twelve stained glass windows, representing the twelve astrological signs. She was stunned by the details of the art explaining their complexion. At the last window at the end of the balcony, Laurie found her sign, the Libra. Right next to it was an enormous statue of Mother Mary holding baby Jesus. Whereas Mary's face was in front of her on the second floor, her feet were on the first floor. Laurie could see the priest entering in front and greet the audience.

Laurie went to sit in the front row, thus having a perfect view of the priest and all the people sitting on the first floor. She was fascinated by the representation of the statue, suggesting Mother Mary undeniably belonged to the two-dimensional world. A young man came and sat down not far behind her. The two of them were the only congregants on the second floor, and Laurie felt she was exactly where she was meant to be.

The priest introduced the group of chorists and went to sit down. The chorists began to sing and right away, incredibly, Laurie felt her heart fill up in an inexplicable way. The feeling was so amazing that she looked up to Heaven, looking at where the sound of music, and the choir's emotions were going. With tears of happiness, she saw with new eyes, the beautiful painting of gods and angels drawn on the vaulted ceiling of the church. In a moment of grace, those paintings of gods seemed to be the physical representation of the astrological signs!

Laurie, who recently had thought nobody remembered about the gods, was thrilled to realize her community, her ancestors who built that church, must have known about their existence and painted them on a sacred place so people would remember. *Why didn't I ever hear about the gods before? Does everyone else know but me?* Exhausted, she greeted the young man next to her and leaned on the fence in front of her, watching the choir below and listened to the theatrical music that suggested a battle between good and evil. Following the wonderful mixed emotions; sometimes pain, sometimes happiness, Laurie simply let her big tears fall freely, reaching the first floor.

At intermission, the young man greeted Laurie and the two of them began to chat. While the boy was telling Laurie and pointing at which one of the singers was his mother, strangely Laurie had in mind that somehow, this boy was her brother. "I don't know you much, but I already love you." Laurie told the boy spontaneously, and with a large smile.

She felt she was in a higher dimension, and understood all souls were connected to each other, like brothers and sisters, having only one mother and one father, before coming to Earth to live a physical life. But before knowing what she meant, the boy quickly left saying he needed to go and grab something.

Serene, Laurie admired the place. Right in the middle of everything, at the level of her sight, was a huge ball-like light fixture that gave her the impression it was the representation of the sun. All along the central aisle, there were all sizes of other light fixtures. She analyzed the possibility, *Could it be a representation of the planets, and the solar system?* Some of them were bigger than others and the light fixtures were all aligned, which reminded her of the real planet's alignment and the vision of the aliens looking for Earth. Powerless, Laurie looked down at the crowd below. The people were all dazzled and attentive to the choir in front of them that had started to sing again with even more intensity as if it was to reassure and protect humanity on Earth. Laurie was euphoric, listening and cherishing the vibration of each soul chanting, as well as the sound of the music coming from the huge pipe organ, that eventually went their way higher up to the Gods.

The boy returned and waved kindly at Laurie who seemed moved by the show. She let herself be lulled by the emotions and special vibrations she felt in her own way, as if the angels were also taking part in this invocation.

When the choir finished, both spectators went their way down together, sharing how they enjoyed the songs. They shook hands before going on their way. Laurie took the time to chat with some members of the choir. They told her they had visited quite a few churches, but this one was one of the greatest they had the pleasure of singing for. Proud of her favorite church, those comments reinforced Laurie's belief that this place could be Jesus's sanctuary.

Laurie returned home feeling her soul fulfilled. She sat next to Brandon who stopped watching TV and asked, with an angry tone, where she was during the last two hours.

"I went to church. What are you watching?" she asked, changing subject, not in a mood to explain anything since it was becoming too difficult to explain what she was going through.

In the middle of the night, still unable to fall asleep, Laurie was listening to the noise of the rain banging on the roof and the windows, as well as the sound of the wind blowing intensely. She opened the curtain, returned to get comfortable in her bed and relished the show that was presented to her through the patio door. With the light of the moon, she looked at the clouds moving rapidly. They began to take forms when a herd of horses came to life. More clouds appeared on top of them, and were taking the form of men, seated on their beasts. The wind still blew intensely. The clouds were moving and transforming rapidly as the horses and the men began to run across fields, mountains, countries, fighting with guns and canons, which were presented with the lightning and the thunder far away. With the chant of nature, Laurie admired this phenomenon until she believed she was witnessing a magnificent story from the gods about the human histories. Honored, she didn't want to miss any moment of this splendid show. Laurie didn't move one bit while staring at the patio window and feeling all sorts of emotions.

The storm quietly finished after a long hour, leaving place for what seemed to Laurie to be an unbelievable Earth cleaning. Many small clouds with the shapes of spaceships, driven by goddesses, were taking turns going down close to Earth. Those clouds were getting bigger as they seemed to be siphoning negative energy from the Earth. Then, at the speed of light, they went up and reached the outside atmosphere.

Laurie could never have imagined such a scenario, but she had the capacity to believe and appreciate. Amazed, she believed this phenomenon was an award to the glorious choral prayers during the evening at the church. Moved, she thanked the singers and the angels for cleaning the human mess on Earth.

***

Laurie had not slept for four days, and she was too disconnected from physical reality to realize her body needed to sleep. She was telling Brandon she was fine, but because he had an appointment that he couldn't delay, for safety, he had taken Laurie to her brother's house for the afternoon. Unfortunately, Laurie's mental health was getting worse because many of her realities were mixing rapidly and more deeply.

With her brother, the alien topic resurfaced. Laurie was pleased to tell him she had discovered his mystery, "I saw you and Mathilde on Friday night at the Irish bar. You borrowed the physical body of two men and came to sit with us."

"What?" Patrick said with some kind of patience trying to understand what she meant.

"You both mutated into someone else's body before entering inside the resto-bar."

Laurie was proud to tell him she recognized them even if they had tried to be incognito. But Patrick answered nothing because to him, it was impossible.

He turned cold staring at his little sister thinking she was making fun of him. And he didn't like her to include Mathilde in her joke. But his cold look activated another reality to Laurie which was from the movie she watched last night; *We need to talk about Kevin*. A strange fiction story about a boy with a mental illness who had once pierced his little sister's eye... not thinking of how her brother could react, she said freely,

"I think you just punctured my eye."

"What are you talking about?" he asked intrigued.

"You just punctured my eye. I can only see with one eye!"

"Well frankly!"

Patrick asked her to put her hand on one eye, then on the other, to prove to her she could still see. And he continued, "How could I have punctured your eye if you can still see?"

Slowly, Laurie was coming back to reality, but this feeling was so strong, and she apparently was able to see in this world, the idea that it could be the work of the alien began to make *his* way.

"Patrick, I'm not blaming you for piercing my eye. I know I don't have a scar or trauma, but guess why? Do you remember when we were kids and we thought we saw an alien spaceship in our neighborhood? I believe that day, the aliens operated on me and installed a special lens in my eye! I don't know why, but it's thanks to their technology that my operation is invisible!" Laurie was trying to explain her new reality.

Patrick added nothing and walked further into the house. For him, it was illogical. Laurie joined him in order to continue to tell him her thoughts, but aggressively he turned to her. He was visibly angry as his eyes turned red. He said, "Nothing that you are saying makes sense."

He looked at his sister with contempt. Unfortunately, Laurie was convinced his eyes were red not because he was sad, but because she was now capable of detecting the evil. In her reality, the alien who came to visit her in her room two days ago, was orchestrated in fact to activate the special incrusted device that had been sleeping in her since her childhood. *I'm now capable to detect the evil in people's thoughts...*

Calm, Emily asked her sister-in-law to sit at the table and talk to her. She listened to Laurie telling the links between Patrick and the aliens until Brandon arrived. He came to pick her up earlier than expected because of the unfortunate dispute between the brother and the sister. Laurie left his home without even listening to the insults her brother was telling her. She told Brandon, who stayed neutral, "Obviously, my brother didn't like when I told him that I see evil in him!"

From then on, worried to say offending words, Laurie stayed quiet for the most part of the evening. That night, when Brandon left for work, Laurie went to the third room and started to move stuff around. Not quite understanding what she was doing, she did it anyway believing it had a meaning for another parallel world.

In the morning, when Brandon returned from work, he was shaken to see Laurie who didn't seem to have slept, and had certainly made some changes in the apartment. He kept his calm and asked her if she wanted to take a bath while he would do an errand. She thought it was a great idea and hurried to run a bath.

Brandon left the apartment and drove to the police station. He explained to Officer Alan about Laurie's situation and added, "My girlfriend has an appointment with her doctor today, but I don't think she will want to go. What should I do? She needs help."

Officer Alan answered, "We cannot do anything without her consent. But if she wants to hurt herself or someone, call us and we will come right away."

In the meantime, in the bathtub, Laurie's mind was resurfacing to the story of the comic Asterix and Obelix. Without premeditation, she was Cleopatra taking a milk bath with her huge cat next to her. While the Egyptian population was building pyramids, Laurie sang the way she remembered Cleopatra singing in the comic; with a pitch voice, her proud rolled-up nose in the air while scrubbing her arms with soap. Joyfully, she was changing her voice to sing the lion part.

Once Laurie realized her skin was pruney, she went to lay down in her bed. As she left one room to get to the other, she left the comic world and merged into the physical world. She noticed this weird change but kept going, not able to change anything. She was now in an unknown human body, entering a pyramid, and laid down into an Egyptian tomb. She covered her entire naked body under the blankets. Through the tiny holes of the blanket, she was able to see a little bit of the outside. She realized she had difficulty breathing but didn't move, trying to understand the meaning of this phenomenon. It seemed she had experienced this moment before.

Everything went black and she felt like a prisoner; then her spirit was in the sky. Some stars shone intensely, and their disposition seemed to be a clear map that would show her the exit. As her mind returned to her body, she saw the same map drawn on her body; instead of stars, it was her freckles. Under the comforter, she couldn't see outside anymore. The tomb she was in seemed to be hidden deeper into the pyramid. She wanted help, but she was incapable of yelling. Between realities, she heard the people who were doing construction in the apartment below, but felt she was trapped in the pyramid and the noise suggested, instead, that people were searching for her, but were lost in this incredible labyrinth.

Finally, she heard Brandon coming up the stairs calling her name. Laurie was crying under the blanket trying to find a way out. Somehow, she managed to follow the direction of her birthmark, and found the courage to get out from the blanket just before Brandon entered the room.

"Why are you crying?" Brandon asked in disbelief.

"I was trapped under the blanket," Laurie said honestly.

"You should get dressed," Brandon said, leaving her alone in the room.

Confused, but happy because she was saved, Laurie unzipped what was covering her nicer dresses and put on her prettiest summer dress. By doing so, she stepped into the Cinderella story. She went to the kitchen and suggested Brandon to throw a party for the kids. "I want to organize a ball for my niece and my friend's kids, as if they were princesses and princes." But Brandon disagreed and his eyes turned rapidly to red. Unfortunately, Laurie immediately associated him as the mad mother-in-law in the story of Cinderella. Nevertheless, she asked Brandon to help her sweep the floor for the party, but Brandon categorically refused and immediately Laurie felt anger rising in her. She wrongly accused him that he never helps her with the household, and she walked out to the balcony to calm down.

Outside, standing up on the third-floor balcony, Laurie felt better. She had the feeling all of nature and the birds' chants were freeing her. Jubilant, she moved her hips and looked at the movement of her princess dress catching in the wind. Proud of her dress with small straps, tight under her chest with a black crinoline under the fabric to give volume to the dress, she began to whistle at the birds, to share her joy with them.

Laurie cherished that moment. But inside, Brandon was worried, thinking his tired girlfriend might try to fly like a bird. Nervous, he joined Laurie and asked her to follow him inside. He had red and swollen eyes. Never did Laurie think it was because he was tired from working all night. No, she thought even more it was her device, her "laser eye" that had once more been activated. Laurie saw in Brandon's eyes negativity such as impatience or the need to control. *He wants to control me because he couldn't stand to see me happy!* Laurie was irritated and all this control had to stop. She spoke aggressively, "No, I won't get in! Leave me alone or I will slap you."

Terribly surprised by her reaction, Brandon shouted for the first time, "You're crazy." He took his cell phone and added, "I'm going to film you, you're not normal." He went inside and Laurie helped him slam the door between the two of them. Brandon immediately called the police.

"Officer Alan here. How may I help you?"

Proud, feeling she had repelled this evil, Laurie resumed her peaceful position on the balcony and looked around. There was a couple arguing in the building across the street and two police cars were arriving and parked in front of her building. Oddly, not in the mood of being curious with a neighbor being arrested, Laurie went inside. She grabbed her broom and continued sweeping to clean the place before the kids would arrive for the ball.

She was so deep in her thoughts that she was surprised to see three police officers following Brandon and entering the kitchen. As Laurie looked at them scanning the room, she was astonishingly impressed about how tall, big, and how strong the officers were. Irrationally, she immediately believed they were avatars, and wondered what the people inside them looked like.

Laurie felt so grateful thinking, in a wrong way, that they had come to free her from Brandon (from Cinderella's mother-in-law). "Come in," she said with the broom in her hand. "I wanted to sweep the floor before I throw a party for my friends' children, that he doesn't want," while pointing at Brandon.

The giant avatar Léonie asked Laurie if children often come to her house. "Of course," Laurie replied proudly while inviting her to take a tour of the apartment. With one look, agent Léonie confirmed to her partners she would question her. Agent Alan stayed with Brandon; while the third agent went outside and called the ambulance.

After a few questions, agent Léonie asked Laurie directly if she would like to accompany her to the hospital for an evaluation. The professional way the agent spoke helped Laurie leave the magical word and return closer to reality. With tears in her eyes, Laurie agreed to follow her.

"Very well. Would you like to bring something with you?" Léonie asked, seeming to be affected by feelings of sadness or incomprehension towards Laurie.

Still dressed in her prettier summer dress, Laurie put on her flip-flops, and picked up her leather coat. She felt rebellious, strong, and courageous as she walked in front of Brandon. In a short time, Laurie went from being a victim to being a combatant. She believed she had a mission, and it was to defend the victims of control abuse. *Why do I have a "laser eye" if it's not to use it!*

There was an ambulance in front of the apartment, and this was Laurie's ride to the hospital. She entered the back of the vehicle with paramedic Alexis who checked her vital signs. On their way, from the back window, Laurie was looking at Brandon following them in his white van.

~ 25 ~

Craziness or on a Special Mission?

The ambulance stopped in front of an emergency door that Laurie had never seen before. Suspicious and aggressive, she asked impatiently, "Which way are we going?" like she was on a mission of saving victims.

Agent Alan showed her the way, and Laurie took the lead. Once they reached the sixth floor, agent Alan asked Brandon and Laurie to wait in the small waiting room. Hesitant, as she got into the waiting room, she vaguely remembered she had an appointment with her Doctor on June 11 at about this hour. She put her leather coat on, and it helped her to feel invincible, then she leaned on the windowsill and looked at the view of Aliville city.

Brandon had rarely seen his girlfriend behave like this. He asked her what she was thinking.

"I don't want to neither talk to you nor look at you. I feel so strong and powerful that I'm afraid I could hurt you with the weapon I have in my eye." After a while, still uninterested in chatting with Brandon, Laurie sensed her doctor was coming. Indeed, Dr. Dion arrived and asked Laurie to follow her, but Laurie didn't move. Just now, she was remembering Brandon and Dr. Dion had a deal to increase her medication a few weeks ago, and despite her refusal...

"Why don't you turn around?" Dr. Dion asked after a few seconds.

Afraid of not being able to control her new weapon, Laurie's solution was to keep her eyes closed. "I'm blind," she told her without turning around.

Brandon let go a sigh of disbelief, which upset Laurie even more.

"I'm not ready to follow you."

"All right Laurie. Come join me in my office when you're ready."

Dr. Dion left, and Brandon also leaned on the edge of the window next to Laurie. He seemed calmer, which helped Laurie to share with him the new mission she thought she had to accomplish.

"Do you see that hole in the brick chimney in front of us?" Laurie asked while pointing to the roof of another part of the hospital. Brandon nodded yes. "Do you remember, I told you about the visit of an alien in my room. That I had a feeling he had inserted a laser in my eye?" Uncertain, Brandon listened attentively without interrupting Laurie who continued, "I know now why. Soon, when the planets will all be aligned, I will have to destroy this hole to prevent the entry of bad grey aliens into our world."

Brandon seemed interested and calm when he reminded Laurie, "Can we discuss this with Dr. Dion? She's waiting for us in her office." Calmer, Laurie agreed and followed Brandon.

Dr. Dion was talking with agent Léonie in the corridor. Laurie wasn't pretending to be blind anymore but became suspicious when she saw her doctor with red eyes. *Can she be mean?* Uncomfortable at the thought of being alone with her and Brandon in the office, she quickly asked agent Léonie, "Can you please accompany me to my appointment? I don't want to be alone with them." Surprised by this request, Léonie looked at Dr. Dion, who looked back at her signaling it was okay, and she should come.

Destabilized, but confident, she entered the doctor's office first and before she sat down, Laurie aggressively took a picture frame that was standing on the desk. She wanted to understand why the doctor had red eyes and what she was hiding. She wanted to confront her, push her to reveal her real identity behind her portrayal of a doctor. *Perhaps she's hiding victims?* But Dr. Dion didn't appreciate Laurie being disrespectful to her. She took back her family photo with some authority and Laurie immediately felt ashamed for being disrespectful, coming back to reality.

Brandon began telling the doctor, "This morning, she wanted to organize a ball and she wanted to invite fairies. And now, she's saying she has a weapon in her eye..." Laurie wasn't part of the conversation anymore. She no longer had the strength, and she was mentally and physically exhausted. She let them chat while feeling confident with Léonie who stood in front of the door.

After a while, Brandon helped his girlfriend to get up as she agreed to go rest. As Laurie was taking her time walking, she had already forgotten where she was going. She asked to stop at the chapel. In this reassuring place, Laurie was telling all kinds of stories. Then Brandon finally looked at his watch and said, "Laurie, it's time to go." Thinking he was referring to the planet's line-up phenomenon that was about to happen, Laurie followed him. She stopped at the first window near the elevator and leaned comfortably while waiting to watch the event. She had her eyes wide open thinking she was about to witness the destruction of the door where bad grey aliens would try to enter our Galaxy.

After a few minutes, Brandon asked her if she was ready to go to her room. Once again, Laurie was confused hearing about the room but the idea of going to rest her exhausted body enchanted her. And since she hadn't seen any signs of a coming event yet, Laurie concluded she misinterpreted the timing which would be later.

She peacefully followed her boyfriend, until the end of the corridor and when they entered the last room, the one that was previously occupied by Pascal, she asked, "Where is Pascal? What am I doing here?" Brandon didn't answer anything, and Laurie was remembering vaguely Pascal's body in a fetal position, as well as when she thought he was baby Jesus during her walk as the Three Wise Men.

She was deep in her thoughts while Brandon helped her to put on the hospital robe. When he was leaving, she asked again panicking, "What am I doing here?" Brandon's eyes were filled with tears as he turned back to Laurie, hugged her, kissed her, and told her he will come back soon.

Nurses began to enter the room as Brandon left, wiping away his tears. Seven nurses, almost all in white uniforms were approaching Laurie who kept her position straight in the middle of the room. She took a deep breath imagining herself surrounded with powerful energies. She felt strong and ready to fight if she had to. Threateningly, she looked at the 'guards' who seemed afraid to approach her, which encouraged her to believe more in her power.

Finally, the first nurse approached Laurie showing her the pills she should be taking. But Laurie didn't like her controlling attitude. *She wants to drug me!* Feeling trapped, Laurie looked at her with a menacing look as not to approach any closer. Then Marc, a mediator that Laurie appreciated meeting during her first hospitalization, was smiling and moving quietly towards her. He was holding white straps in a way to show them to Laurie so as not to frighten her. Laurie felt like a wild animal, a dragon perhaps, but the fire inside her faded away while looking at the kindly man coming her way. Laurie had thought previously of him, he could be an angel because of his white immaculate uniform and his kind personality. She let him come closer to her sensing he was telling her; *Let us help you.*

Laurie lowered her guard while understanding these white straps were in fact an alternative to medication. "I'm okay with the restraint straps, but I don't want to take the pills." Marc and the other nurses approached closer to Laurie ready to jump on her if they thought it was necessary. But they didn't need to. Laurie's reality had just switched in a nano second. She was seeing this moment from higher up, outside of her body. In that frozen moment, Laurie recalled Pascal, who had been the last patient confined in this room, but also, he had a sixth sense. Irrationally, she proclaimed inwardly, *Pascal was an alien!* In this way of thinking, the seven people wearing white uniforms, were working in a laboratory for Nasa and it wasn't really a hospital room. *Pascal was supposed to go into the universe and complete the mission. But something went wrong since he is no longer here. And now they want me to go?*

Laurie believed that the mission had been interrupted and they were now asking her to go to space and destroy, somehow, the galaxy door. *Why not? An intelligent being came to me, revealed his way of communication, and inserted a powerful weapon into my body! Not to mention that several times over the last few weeks, I had experienced weightlessness during my out-of-body travels in space! Yes, I could be the one fit for this mission!*

Back in her body, Laurie nodded to Marc that she accepted the mission.

On the verge of fainting, she let them grab her and moved her to the bed. When she woke up, the seven professionals were around, looking at her while Marc was tying the last strap. Thinking they were preparing her to go to space, she moved every part that was tied in order to feel comfortable for the mission. She told Marc about the last strap being too tight, so Marc immediately loosened it some.

Between the two realities she was in, Laurie interpreted the worried look on the faces of the Nasa professionals as to mean; *We are running out of time, and you are the last chance to achieve the mission.* She smiled at Mark who was about to inject a liquid into her left thigh. In Laurie's reality, they tied her up to make sure her body stayed on Earth during her mission in space! Laurie nodded confirming he could proceed; thinking the mission would probably be more intense than her previous travel to space. She took a deep breath while Marc injected the liquid into her body.

The place had become deserted and dark. Waiting for the mission to begin, Laurie was proud to have been chosen. Imagining her fire dragon flying into space, she longed with all her heart to fulfill and succeed in this obligation. Yet tears flowed down as she was hoping her soul would make a comeback.

***

When Laurie woke up, her body was no longer tied up. She felt rested but confused. She had no memory of how she had been propelled into space, which made her doubt about Nasa and the mission, until slowly, she realized the seven people dressed in white were in fact nurses who had injected her with a liquid drug rather than giving her a pill! *Of course, they knew I wouldn't take pills!*

Laurie laughed at herself realizing how much imagination she had lately. And she agreed that a calming medication was necessary to help her calm down. The door opened and Laurie's imagination intertwined again with the story of Cinderella. *It's my fairy godmother!* Laurie thought while welcoming Angela, her godmother entering the room like any other time, smiling, not worried about the situation, and happy to see Laurie. She sat next to her goddaughter and asked her what happened. But Laurie didn't know where to start, so Angela asked with an amused look, "Brandon says you wanted to organize a party and invite the fairies. Is that true?"

With a step back, Laurie realized how unrealistic it sounded. She smiled back a little bit ashamed, but ready to defend her point, "I wanted to organize a ball for the kids. I felt there was some kind of magic energies around me, and I wanted them to feel it, too."

Angela laughed spontaneously, and Laurie enjoyed her way of de-dramatizing the situation. Remembering Angela's presence all through her life until now, Laurie embraced the picture that was presented in her mind of Angela with a magic wand. *Of course, she is my fairy godmother!*

***

During her second hospitalization, her visits with others had not been so great though. The doctors, Laurie's father, Brandon, and Arianne had all tried to convince her to take the medication, but Laurie refused, arguing that it was impossible one pill could filter her thoughts. She had put a stop to their visits to avoid arguments and to avoid postponing her way out of the hospital. She had not appreciated her father's last visit because he didn't accept the idea that Laurie wanted to see Tim, her energy teacher. He thought Tim and his energy class were the reason Laurie had become 'crazy.'

But Laurie told her father with an arrogant tone, "I must protect him from people like you! People who don't believe in what they can't see!"

With Arianne, it was the first time Laurie was sarcastic with her, "I don't think medication will help me say or not say something. Maybe you should re-educate me?" But when she was alone in her hospital room, she released all of her suffering. She cried feeling the pain of the disappointment she was causing. She feared that her loved ones may no longer love her.

During the two following weeks, trying to get over it, Laurie participated in activities, spent time with Dominic playing chess, with Sébastien reading his poems. She listened to Mr. Mathieu's stories, took care of

Mrs. Rita and her skin infection by applying cold water towels to it. She read stories with Seasol and other new patients. Laurie seemed to be normal to them, however, per moment, her thoughts continued juggling between past lives or parallel worlds that seemed to happen mostly in the morning after waking up.

To move on, Laurie finally asked her doctor to leave the hospital. Dr. Dion allowed her discharge saying, "Still, we don't have a diagnosis about your condition. It could be schizophrenia, or bipolar, but we don't have enough data to confirm it. Only time will tell. You seem better than when you arrived, but you also seem like when we gave your first discharge one month ago. And unfortunately, you needed to come back!"

Later that day, with Brandon on her side, at the nurse counter, Laurie received her belongings. When she opened the big white bag, she was in shock to find her most beautiful dress. Painfully, she remembered her ride from home to the hospital, and the inappropriate way she was dressed when she last checked in. But the memory of the only other time she had worn this beautiful dress was even more painful; it was at her mother's funeral, four years ago.

~ 26 ~

What Needed to Be Witnessed

Monday, June 25, 2012

Laurie was discharged from her second hospitalization and was back in her apartment. It felt like déjà vu. Only this time, she was aware that she could return to floor six, in psychiatry, at any time as it happened before.

It was her first night at home, she was lying on her bed, and the alarm clock showed two a.m. Brandon was gone to work, and Laurie couldn't sleep. Without a warning, her mind was again in space looking at the Universe. With fantasy in her vision, lines were formed from specific stars. The constellation of Centurion, which Laurie knew more as the Sagittarius zodiac, appeared clearly in front of her.

As she admired this amazing vision, Laurie wondered what she knew about Sagittarius. Quickly, she recalled her mother having this zodiac sign while leaving her last earthly life! The phenomena continued and the drawing of the half-man, half centaur began to move and appeared in 3D. It was magical. The Sagittarius became alive and stood in the middle of the Universe. She was in admiration while looking at his four robust legs and his strong and straight body holding firmly his stretched bow in the immensity of the cosmos. He had a sharp look while looking at the tip of his rigid arrow. Surprisingly, it seemed like he was getting ready to shoot at a target.

From an unknown place in the galaxy, Laurie was witnessing the tray of gas, the Milky Way in slow motion, moving around the Sagittarius, as it was following its natural rotation in the Universe. Eventually, a distinguished fume of dark purple, pink, and gray colors appeared in her field of view. Following the tray of gas rotation, Laurie was paying close attention to the movement, and the mass, which is usually called "The Black Hole." *This mass is about to be perfectly aligned with Sagittarius's arrow!* Astonished, she was thinking. *Could it be?* Out of nowhere, Laurie felt like it was her mom's spirit telling her; *Yes, and look, it's happening now!*

That powerful energy of Sagittarius divinely unloaded its sharp arrow like it had always been prepared for that special alignment. The magnificent and unique arrow perfectly reached the exact middle of the Black Hole and continued his way straight inside of what seemed to be another powerful energy, slowly siphoning our atmosphere and our stars. Laurie was more speechless by this phenomenon because she couldn't ever imagine such a scenario; in the Galaxy, a constellation was shooting at the Black Hole!

She wondered. *Why? Is that celestial performance meant to destroy that Black Hole, to protect our Universe and to seal from coming in or going out? Laurie imagined it was* to prevent the invasion of the grey men coming from other Galaxies, or vice versa, to stop the phenomenon of siphoning the stars of our Galaxy.

As she waited for answers, the current phenomenon was continuing. Next to the excited Sagittarius, other lines were formed from the stars of the constellation of Orion, and Orion also quickly came to life.

Laurie was more than captivated in front of this huge 3D image. In this particular moment, in weightlessness, she didn't need to breathe, she wasn't feeling her pulse, and didn't need to blink an eye. She wasn't hearing the noise; she was feeling it, living it. She was feeling Orion's calmness, and the majesty of its movements. Ready to defend the Sagittarius, Orion also rose bigger in the immense galaxy. He firmly held his sword in his right hand and carried his huge shield to protect himself and Sagittarius, from projectiles coming from the impact. Laurie was impressed to see this legend alive, joining this phenomenon, standing alongside the Sagittarius.

Laurie then looked at the tiny but numerous little black projectiles from the impact, coming towards the two giant fighters. In front of this presentation, Laurie would have laughed but she couldn't express any feeling in that atmosphere. Or was it the seriousness of the event? The projectiles were moving slowly toward the immensity of Orion's shield. They were so small that Laurie couldn't tell if the projectiles were possible debris of stars from the impact of the arrow or was it spaceships of unwanted grey men who might have crossed before the door of the Black Hole was destroyed. Or a mix of both; debris and spaceships?

Unfortunately, the vision ended without giving her more answers. Laurie was back in her physical body, while breathing calmly, considering the phenomenon she had just witnessed. A reality that belongs to the greatest form of life.

She felt privileged, and honored for this amazing vision that helped her acknowledge the existence of those gods, and their powerful energy all over the galaxy. Hugging her pillow hard, she just wanted to be loved and held by them. She wanted to be as celestial as them. While in those thoughts, her heart immediately accelerated as they were sharing with her that she was born from one of these constellations. As she had learned not too long ago, humans were children of the Sun and the Earth. But the energy/soul were children of the Solar System—the constellations.

She heard the myth of gods from different epoch and cultures, which entered into her mind. The Mayans and Egyptians believed in gods in the sky. Yet, Laurie understood what they were seeing: their energies, their strength, their complexity, their essence. She felt sad their realities faded away over time till the point people forgot about them. *What happened?*

She briefly remembered her mom, Mr. Gilbert, and his wife; they had to carefully speak about cosmic science because it wasn't welcomed in society. She remembered her close friends making fun of people expressing their beliefs in those subjects, so it was also her reason she never really tried to talk about topics outside the "normal." The image of the Black Hole came to her mind to show another kind of powerful energy siphoning life and intelligence.

***

In the morning, Brandon asked his girlfriend how she slept. "Good," she simply answered. Since that moment, she strongly felt the need to call Mrs. Rondeau. Perhaps because she had been referred to her by Mr. Gilbert, Laurie's massage therapist, who once had talked about Orion's sword and its powerful force of healing, Laurie felt deeply that she would be cured if she could meet with her. She had met her once a couple of months ago and she had been impressed by her great mediumship; the way she seemed to communicate with invisible energies who told her what Laurie needed to know.

Remembering Mrs. Rondeau and her gift, Laurie was amused, thinking, *Why didn't I think about meeting her before?* As an answer, a voice inside her seemed to suggest; *if I had met her before, she would have healed me, and I wouldn't have witnessed what happened last night in the greatest level with the constellations!* Without waiting, Laurie called her.

At first, the lady said she was full with appointments that day. Laurie waited a few seconds wishing deeply the lady would change her mind and find time for her. Then Mrs. Rondeau finally said; "I must see you! Can you come at 5:30 today?" Relieved, Laurie thanked the lady, confirming she would be there.

Mrs. Rondeau opened the door before Laurie knocked. She greeted her patient while analyzing her. She asked her to sit down on the comfortable chair to her right, and sat in front of Laurie, smiling with an intriguing look.

Strangely, Laurie was feeling her own energy growing. She felt powerful and had the impression that Mrs. Rondeau felt it, too. As she was being observed, Laurie seemed to understand the universe around her. How it works for efficient psychics, or gifted humans to get to know people's secrets in order to help them by guiding them. *It's MY inner presence that shows what the lady needs to know to help me with my issue!* Laurie was amazed to realize that her inner presence was trying to get in contact with Mrs. Rondeau's soul.

To begin, they chatted lightly. Laurie felt tired. She felt her spirit detaching from her body as her energy was spreading throughout the room. She had to concentrate to understand what the lady was asking. She thought Mrs. Rondeau would tell her something like, *Wow Laurie, you are so powerful!* But instead, the lady asked her what happened to her lately. Back to reality, feeling an intense stress in her belly, and the fast beating of her heart, Laurie began to rapidly describe (with extreme emotions) the phenomenon she went through and the visions she had.

Mrs. Rondeau's facial expression changed as the speaker was going too fast and her speech was incoherent. She interrupted her, "Wait a minute!" and she put her hand in front of her at the level of the belly, so as to cut the energy between them. In the invisible, Laurie saw her energy deflect in front of the lady's "shield" she had just installed between their two bodies...

Mrs. Rondeau asked her to calm down and Laurie was impressed by how her entire body immediately reacted to the order. Calmer, Laurie kept talking about her adventure for quite a while, until Mrs. Rondeau moved in her chair showing the session was over.

"What am I supposed to do now?" Laurie asked as she got up. With tears of despair, she couldn't believe that it was over. *I don't feel like I'm healed!* Laurie didn't move one step. Instead, she took a deep breath and immediately asked her inner presence to share the best vision possible in order to bring this lady to find out what to do to cure her. In this surge of deep desire, a pure white light appeared in Laurie's world, and she felt a spark of love saying; *don't worry, we are here, and we will help you because you asked for it.*

Mrs. Rondeau began to look at Laurie differently. She seemed intrigued as if she had just discovered something important. "The meeting is over Laurie. But I can't let you go like this. I'm going to try something on you if you don't mind?" She moved further from the chairs in order to find enough room to turn around her patient, who was standing straight, and barely breathing; wishing the magic would work on her.

Since the few energy classes she had taken with Tim and some reiki moments with Mr. Gilbert, Laurie had learned how to connect her root chakra with the core of the Earth and her crown chakra to the sky. However, for the last couple months, she had completely forgotten about the chakras and the roots.

Mrs. Rondeau walked away in order to take a full picture of Laurie, then walked around her still with her right hand pressed on her belly.

Mrs. Rondeau asked Laurie if she knew how to connect herself to the Earth and to the sky. Laurie immediately proceeded and she felt an immense mass of energy separate at the level of her belly. The upper part went directly and quickly to the sky while the other part traveled towards the ground, under her feet, and began to spread robustly in all directions like the roots of a huge hungry tree.

Laurie was feeling powerful when she heard Mrs. Rondeau speaking in an alarmed tone. "No! Directly to the core of the Earth and to the Sun!" At the very moment, when Laurie imagined the core of the Earth, all the roots instantly began to move in that same direction and vigorously clung to it in one straight line. The energy of the upper body did the same and clung in one straight line to the Sun.

Incredibly, at this right moment, Laurie felt completely straight, anchored and well balanced.

"Yes, like that Laurie." Mrs. Rondeau approached and began to make movements with her hands while moving around her. It reminded Laurie of the incantation she had received when she was a teenager and Mother Mary had come to protect her. Laurie's eyes were closed, and she was experiencing the benefit of Mrs. Rondeau treatment. She felt her body to be well balanced, her emotions were living in the right places and her ideas were much clearer. In a thought (much like a vision) she saw her soul smiling at her, winked at her saying; *You should no longer worry. From now on, everything will be fine!*

When Laurie opened her eyes, Mrs. Rondeau looked at her attentively and, in her eyes, Laurie perceived that she had rarely seen a case like hers, commenting, "Well, I think you should feel better now."

Extremely grateful, Laurie thanked her with all her heart. "You're right. I'm feeling better already. I sincerely believe that you have healed me."

As she left the residence, Laurie felt sure she was finally back with full control of herself, her thoughts, and actions. Hopeful, she was happy to get back to Brandon, looking forward to seeing her family, her friends, soon her community and her coworkers.

***

A week later, still feeling great and well balanced, Laurie met with Mrs. Rondeau with the intention of talking about the treatment she had carried out on her. She needed confirmation of what she thought had happened during their last appointment. Mrs. Rondeau confirmed that it was what Laurie remembered. Yes, she had sensed the power of her energy that had flowed in all directions and anchored straight to the core of the Earth and Sky when she had asked her to take roots. "Honestly, I don't understand why your chakras were all opened. They were not working well. I had to clean and close them."

Laurie confessed she had taken classes on chakra energy. Embarrassed, she admitted she had opened them a few months ago and probably forgotten to close them despite her energy teacher's orders. Mrs. Rondeau then reprimanded her patient by telling her never to open her chakras again. "You don't need to open your chakras to feel the outside. I never opened mine! Otherwise, you now know what happens!"

Laurie left her healer's residence remembering exactly when she had opened her chakras and never closed them after. It was about two months ago, when walking in her neighborhood on a beautiful sunny day, she had offered her help to the Universe with the hope of helping humanity to evolve. It was a few days before the student demonstration that had taken place in her little town.

Laurie also met with Mr. Gilbert to check on another important phenomenon she cherished. She wanted to verify with him if he really saw his divine guide appearing during their last meeting. He positively confirmed, "Yes, and I saw its entirety." He looked enthusiastic, seeming just as reassured as Laurie that he had not been the only one to see the Light Being, and the phenomenon really happened.

A few days later, there was a documentary on television about how the constellations were in motion during the summer months of 2012. It seemed the star at the end of the arrow of Centaurus, the Sagittarius, was passing right in front of the Black Hole of our Galaxy! And the stars of Orion's constellation were right next to him.

***

In conclusion, for some readers, the mental health problem will remain the only reason that caused the disorder in Laurie's actions and thoughts. And they are absolutely right to believe so. She certainly needed help, because she was no longer sleeping, and no longer measured the rationality of her words and actions. Medical help was essential to help her get back to sleep.

She had opened her chakras without knowing how to control them, and she was uprooted from the Earth plane. Although Mrs. Rondeau maintains that Laurie was cured because of her willpower, belief and positivism, Laurie believes that this type of treatment, and other alternative medicines, could be the solution to help people experiencing from similar symptoms to the behaviors described in this story.

After more than 10 years of writing, rewriting, and putting the sequence of events in place, here is Laurie's understanding: because she was healed immediately after having her chakras balanced, she naturally believes that her special episode in 2012, which lasted about 45 days, never relapsed, was the result of her prayer to God... Unsure if the predicted end-of-the-world would happen, she had asked God for help to protect mankind, and help them find their peace and freedom.

Because of her previous experiences with the spiritual world, she believed in a higher force. She had opened her chakras and offered her help to the Universe. As a result, by pure coincidence or not, on the fourth anniversary of her mother's death, her chakras opened more. When she was used as a lightning rod, the energy of the Earth had passed into her and had reached Heaven.

Having her root chakra and the crown chakra fully opened, this led to her soul detaching from her body at times and traveling to other worlds. With the opening of her heart and third eye chakras, she saw, and even came into contact with different beings.

Since she was healed completely the day after her last adventure in space; As she was a spectator of the existence of higher forces (the constellations), somehow, she understood that she had reached the source.

During her writing, remembering the exceptional moments of weightlessness in the Galaxy, she understood that she was both connected to her physical body, as well as, in an inexplicable way, an energy like (a star), she was witnessing the celestial phenomena protecting the Earth and the Galaxy.

Because she had no control and simply let herself be guided, she sincerely believes that she witnessed what the Universe wanted to show her, and make her understand...

These billions of stars in the Galaxy, living in weightlessness in the celestial plane, are intelligent energies and had wanted more. So, the Sun and the Earth, with the influence of the Moon and the planets, created life on Earth; vegetation; then designed physical bodies to be used as vehicles.

A paradise for all, as every religion has tried to teach; God and the Virgin Mary gave birth through the action of the Holy Spirit. The energies of these stars have incarnated on Earth, to live another kind of life in parallel; a place where they can express themselves, grow, evolve freely, each at their own pace, through the eras of linear time. A physical paradise where it is possible to touch, taste, smell, breathe and love.

Do you doubt the phenomenon of reincarnation? Watch a baby being born. His soul is locked up in his new body. Naturally, he learns to eat, to walk, to talk again. He brings his previous experiences, his joys, his fears, his knowledge, his problems unsolved... imprisoned in his etheric body.

For a moment, close your eyes, imagine your physical body disappearing. Who are you? What do you see? Where are you?

Does it seem possible that you are an intelligent energy under your physical body?

On that note, Laurie was very lucky to be cured and to feel no aftereffects despite her incredible adventure. She thanks her loved ones from the bottom of her heart for their help, discretion, support, and unconditional love.

Many thanks to you!

Epilogue

It is important to mention that the author disclaims any responsibility that this reading may cause to the reader. Laurie has her own journey, and the results may not be the same. She does not encourage anyone to imitate the actions described or to stop their medication without their doctor's approval. The purpose of this book is to: open discussions regarding the possible causes of certain mental illnesses, to consider that there are other worlds to ours where other beings live, and to help reconnect with our inner being.

If you enjoyed reading this story, please help me circulate this book so that it reaches as many souls as possible. Give a copy to someone you love. Maybe this reading could help him or her to free themselves or open up to some of those taboo subjects. Please, like and comment positively, or respectfully.

I hope that this story will bring a new approach to healing, and that we can begin to live in balance and enjoy our paradise offered.

Because in my experience, life is so much easier, and beautiful when you know who you are!